Western Region
in the 1960s

6991

Western Region in the 1960s

C.S. HEAPS LL.B.

LONDON
IAN ALLAN LTD

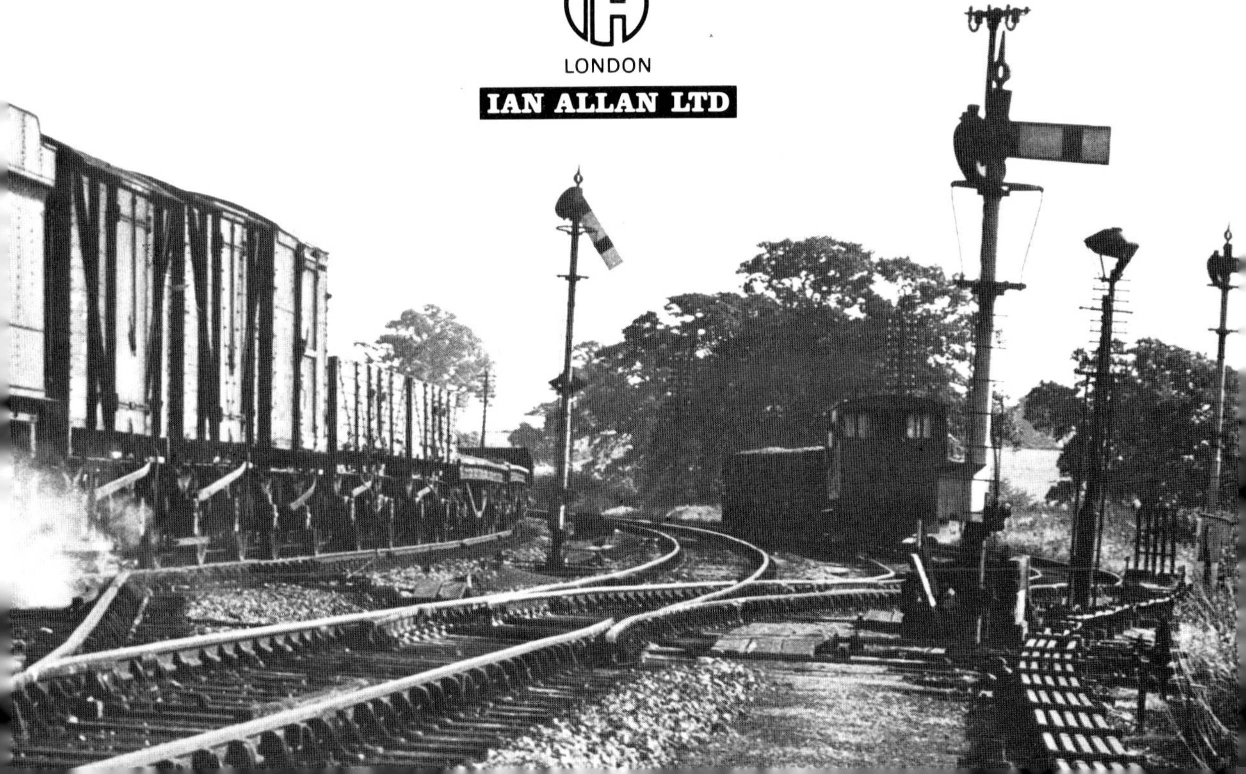

First published 1981

ISBN 0 7110 1126 5

Published by Ian Allan Ltd, Shepperton, Surrey; and printed by Ian Allan Printing Ltd at their works at Coombelands in Runnymede, England

Contents

Foreword

This is a book about a rather special part of the British Railways system — the Western Region. I admit to a bias because I travelled frequently on the 'Western' (the GWR of course) as a child, and spent the first 22 years of my professional career on the Region (1948-1969).

The years 1960 to 1969 were indeed ones of transition for the Western. During that period I was successively District Traffic Superintendent, Birmingham; Divisional Manager, Plymouth and Divisional Manager, London and from my personal knowledge of those interesting years I can confidently assert that the account of that period which follows in words and photographs has been most accurately brought together.

It is important that we should be able to read about change in retrospect as this is a stimulus to us to go forward into the future and to make the changes, which the British Railways system needs if it is to continue to be a leading mode of transport in the remaining years of this century and beyond.

Thus, here you will find described, with wonderful supporting photographs, this important ten year period of change — the accelerating transition from a wagon load freight railway towards a bulk train load system; the growth and development of Inter-City; the end of an era for many rural lines; and all-embracing, the completion of the major transition of the Region's motive power from steam to diesel power — these all come through very effectively in the author's most readable text.

The album could only have been prepared by an author with an abiding and continuing interest in Railways and this Chris Heaps most surely has. He portrays the 'Western' so well, because he had that incomparable advantage of having part of his learning instilled in the very heart of Western territory in Devonshire.

It was in those times of major change in the West Country 1963-1964 that I knew him well. He was President of the Exeter University Railway Society; he was an enthusiastic sponsor of the University train at the end of term; and he even organised a private traffic survey for us, which helped the Region make up its mind to introduce the 'Golden Hind' between Plymouth and London at the time.

You will find that Chris Heaps has provided us with an album, which is authoritative, readable and imaginatively illustrated. Both our memories and our enthusiasm for the 'Western' are enriched by his work, which I warmly commend to you.

David Pattisson
Chief Administration Officer
British Railways Board
London NW1
September, 1980

Introduction

Question: 'Is it occasionally possible to achieve perfection?'
Answer: 'Only on the Great Western, Chairman.'

The answer of the Chairman of the British Railways Board, Mr Peter Parker (as he then was), to a question from the Select Committee on Nationalised Industries on 7 March 1978 speaks volumes for the standing and reputation of the Great Western Railway, which had ceased to exist as a separate entity upon nationalisation over 30 years earlier.

When, in 1948, the GWR had become part of British Railways following the passage of the Transport Act 1947, 112 years of independence came to an end; the employees of the GWR probably resented and feared the new nationalised future more than their counterparts on the London Midland & Scottish, the London & North Eastern and the Southern Railways, companies of mere 25 years' standing.

So strongly did the last General Manager of the GWR, Sir James Milne, fight against the proposals for State ownership that he considered it proper to decline the invitation to act as Chairman of the Railway Executive when formed under the 1947 Act. The Transport Act 1947 was a huge piece of legislation, much of which was not considered in detail by Parliament because the discussions in committee stage were subject to the guillotine procedure. As Michael Bonavia has detailed in his book, *The Birth of British Rail*, the respective spheres of influence of the British Transport Commission, the overall statutory body with responsibility not only for railways but also for roads and waterways, and the Railway Executive were unclear and, from the start, there was tension and uncertainty between the parties not anticipated by the progenitors of the Act.

The Railway Executive, with the task not only of looking to the future but also of running the existing system with the run-down facilities existing after World War 2 — the facilities that had been so unfairly described by Hugh Dalton in the debate in the House of Commons in the 1946 session as 'a poor bag of assets' — had little choice in the short term but to continue the existing practices of the old 'Big Four' companies. Locomotives of pre-nationalised design continued to be built, and on the Western Region — as the Great Western Railway had become — the last 'Castle' class 4-6-0 main line express locomotive, No 7037 *Swindon* was not constructed until November 1950, and the last 0-6-0PT, No 3409, was not delivered until November 1956. An early move was to seek what would now be described as a corporate image and, after experiments, it was decided to paint all main line coaching stock in a 'raspberry and cream' livery and to apply a standard locomotive livery scheme to locomotives of all Regions. The adoption of green livery for main line locomotives other than 8P classification was welcomed by the Western Region, but no true Great Western man would ever admit that the standard blue livery adopted for the most powerful passenger locomotives ever suited the pride of the Great Western Railway, the 'Kings'.

The Great Western was not, however, easily to be defeated and the blue livery was abandoned, to be replaced by GW brunswick green in 1951. By 1955, the greater Regional autonomy permitted by the Transport Act 1953 enabled the Western Region also to abandon standard BR coaching livery (now being changed to maroon) and to reintroduce 'chocolate and cream' coaches on its main-line passenger trains from 1956.

The revival of 'Great Westernism', described by G. Freeman Allen in his work *The Western since 1948* as the 'Great Western Region', began with the restoration of the high-speed (for those days) 'Bristolian', and the reincarnation from York Railway Museum of the famous 4-4-0 *City of Truro* which is credited with the first recorded speed of over 100mph. Chocolate and cream livery was introduced initially on the 'Cornish Riviera Limited', the 'Torbay Express' and the 'Bristolian', but the temptation to extend the traditional livery to all parts of the system led to its adoption by all named trains and the introduction of new named trains for this very purpose. On the West of England main line, the 'Royal Duchy' and 'Mayflower' from Paddington shared tracks beyond Taunton with the 'Cornishman' from Wolverhampton and the 'Devonian' from Bradford. On the South Wales route, the 'Capitals United Express', the 'Red Dragon' and the 'Pembroke Coast Express' were so adorned; the 'Cathedrals Express' and 'Cheltenham Spa Express' enabled passengers from Hereford and Worcester, and Cheltenham, respectively to spend the day in London, and on the Birmingham line the 'Cambrian Coast Express' was joined by the 'Inter-City' — anticipating by some years the marketing brand name of the future — on the run between Paddington and Birmingham (Snow Hill).

By the end of the 1950s green-liveried 'Kings', 'Castles' and other named Great Western-built locomotives hauled chocolate and cream coaches throughout the Region, controlled by lower-quadrant Great Western signals and assisted by the Great Western automatic train control (atc). Even though upper-quadrant signals had been adopted as standard by the other members of the 'Big Four' even before nationalisation, the Western Region continued to manufacture and erect lower-quadrant signals as if nationalisation had never taken place. After nationalisation, the Great Western's atc system was not extended to other Regions (and was ultimately replaced even on the WR) but was superseded by a new BR-designed automatic warning system (aws) which was slowly introduced by British Railways on all main lines.

In contrast, it can be said that by the end of 1969 the Western Region had become a fully integrated part of British Railways, its passenger stock painted in the all-embracing BR blue and grey livery and hauled increasingly by diesel-electric locomotives standard to all Regions and controlled more and more by modern colour-light signalling. The period between 1960 and 1969 — I apologise to purists who maintain that the decade commenced in 1961 — can be seen as the decade of development during which the Western Region ceased looking back to history and began to look forward to the future, to the HST decade that was to follow.

Although the restoration of all things 'Great Western' in the late 1950s no doubt delighted all GWR aficionados, the Region's finances by 1959 were in a sorry state and the Region had an operating deficit of £30m. In an attempt to save the situation and to turn around not only the deficit but the attitude of the Region, Stanley Raymond (later Sir Stanley Raymond: Chairman of the British Railways

Board 1965-7) was appointed as the first non GW-bred General Manager on 1 January 1962, and from that date can the transition of the Western Region to a modern railway be traced.

The transition during the decade of development was brought about in different ways: by new management, new motive power, new rolling stock, new signalling and new timetables. Of these, good management was paramount. Stanley Raymond arrived at Paddington like a new broom, and swept away GWR traditions — often on principle — to introduce his new philosophy. Even before the publication of the Beeching Report in late 1962, the Region had embarked upon a large programme of unremunerative branch line closures, and I personally well remember the shock and horror with which proposals were received for the closure of my local branch line between Helston and Gwinear Road in Cornwall, the first line to be threatened in the county since before World War 2. Strenuous local opposition was presented to the Transport Users' Consultative Committee — all in vain — and such scenes were repeated throughout the Region between 1962 and 1964.

The Beeching closure proposals included many of the ex-Southern Region branch lines in Devon and Cornwall, and the ex-Somerset & Dorset Railway, all of which had come within the Western Region on the boundary revisions operative from 1 January 1963. In this reorganisation the WR lost its control of lines in the Birmingham area, which had previously been intertwined with London Midland Region responsibility; and also disposed of the lines to the north and west stretching into mid-Wales, and the operating deficit that went with them. Before his translation to the British Railways Board in 1963, Raymond also reorganised the traffic management structure of the Region into four Divisions — London, Bristol, Cardiff and Plymouth — and was able to hand over a ship-shape craft to his successor as Chairman of the Western Region Board, Gerald Francis Gisborn Twisleton-Wykeham-Fiennes OBE.

When Raymond had been appointed to the Western Region, its operating deficit of £30,000,000 had been more than one-third of the whole British Railways deficit; within two years the Regional deficit had been halved. Raymond told his successor that he had loved his time on the Western, and Fiennes reveals in his book, *I tried to run a Railway*, that he too very rapidly became 'Western over the years'.

During Fiennes' period of office, the Western Region managed to reach the top of the British Railways punctuality league, as Fiennes improved morale not only of the staff but also of passengers. The question of morale was particularly important at the time of the publication of Dr Beeching's further thoughts on the future of British Railways in 1965, when he recommended the abolition of all railways in Cornwall, the closure of the Berks & Hants main line and the end of the (already rationalised) Salisbury-Exeter route. Local political pressure was inevitable, and strong, when Beeching's views were revealed, but as Fiennes has admitted, his task in defending the future of the Western Region against attacks by West Country MPs and others was greatly assisted by the fact that the Divisional Manager at Plymouth — David Pattisson — had already given evidence of BR plans to retain and improve West Country services by introducing (in the summer timetable of 1964) a new high-speed business 'crack' express — the 'Golden Hind' — between Plymouth and London. I have always enjoyed somewhat proprietary feelings towards the 'Golden Hind', as I understand that one of the factors upon which its introduction was based was the result of a survey by the Exeter University Railway Society (of which I was then President) which had revealed a demand for such a business service. This survey had been organised with the full support of David Pattisson, to whom must go full credit for the resurgence of the West of England services which today form an important part of the Western Region passenger network.

In the event, the Western Region was able to stave off the worst excesses of the Beeching 'Second Report', and during the 1960s managed to improve services steadily but generally, eg by accelerating and extending to Truro (and later to Penzance) the 'Golden Hind', introducing Motorail services to the West Country and Wales, and preserving the rail link to Fishguard by the relatively cheap and simple expedient of converting the Fishguard-Rosslare ferry *St David* to a roll-on roll-off carrier. Anxiety about the future of the main lines 'condemned' by Beeching Part II was partly assuaged by such threatened lines being included in the plans illustrating the 'network for development' published jointly by Stanley Raymond (by then Chairman of the British Railways Board) and The Rt Hon Mrs Barbara Castle MP (Minister of Transport) in March 1967.

When Fiennes was transferred away from the Western Region at the end of 1965 to be Chairman and General Manager of the Eastern Region, with the specific task of amalgamating the Eastern and North Eastern Regions, the Western Region was not yet 'in the black' but Fiennes had high hopes that it would reach that happy state within the next two years. He was replaced at Paddington by Lance Ibbotson, who in turn was followed in 1968 by

John Bonham-Carter, who remained in charge until the end of the decade. These Chairmen and their successors continued to build on the strong foundations laid by Raymond and Fiennes, with the result that the Western Region enjoyed the distinction of providing HST (High Speed Train) 125mph services on all its main lines to South Wales, Bristol and Penzance by the end of the 1970s at a standard of speed and frequency unmatched in Europe.

If the quality of management during the decade of development was paramount, the introduction of new motive power during the first half of the decade was of almost equal importance and, of course, more obvious to the travelling public. At the beginning of 1960, Swindon Works was still building steam locomotives — the last of the Class 9F 2-10-0s, No 92220, *Evening Star*, was not delivered until March 1960 — and 95% of the Region's locomotives were steam, although British Railways had decided, following the 1955 Modernisation Plan, to concentrate in future on building diesel and electric locomotives. Almost inevitably, although not without good reason, the Western Region pursued its own unique policy, by favouring diesel-hydraulic transmission instead of the diesel-electric system adopted by all other Regions. By 1960, in addition to the experimental gas turbine locomotive ordered by the GWR before nationalisation, No 18000 (which was withdrawn in 1961), the first five North British-built 'Warship' A1A-A1A diesel-hydraulic locomotives Nos D600-604 were in service, together with about a dozen of the later Swindon-built B-B 'Warships' in the D800 series (later Class 42). Approximately half-a-dozen Type 2 B-B 1,000hp small diesel-hydraulics in the D6300 class (later Class 22) had also been delivered by North British, but otherwise all main line services and goods services were steam-hauled.

The diesels were first introduced in Devon and Cornwall, the area west of Newton Abbot having been designated as the first area to be dieselised, on the grounds that experience of complete dieselisation could more easily be gained in a relatively self-contained geographical area. They were employed on main-line services such as the 'Cornish Riviera', 'The Royal Duchy', and 'Torbay Express' and, as part of a Laira (Plymouth) based roster, also on the 'Bristolian'. Elsewhere, steam continued to range supreme: all 30 of the mighty 'Kings' remained in service until early 1962, and 'Castle' class 4-6-0 locomotives were still being modernised by the provision of efficient (if ungainly) double chimneys. The 'Kings' themselves had been rejuvenated by the provision of double chimneys between 1955 and 1957.

Within six years, however, steam had been abolished from the Western Region and the locomotive scene transformed.

At the beginning of the decade, the 'King' class locomotives enjoyed a final fling on the Paddington-South Wales service after BR Standard Class 7MT 'Britannias' were transferred away from Cardiff Canton to the London Midland Region; they also dominated the Paddington-Birmingham line expresses immediately before (and occasionally after) the intensive two-hour service to Birmingham was introduced in 1962 during modernisation and electrification of the ex-London & North Western line from Euston to Birmingham. 'Castles' saw service on all WR main lines in the early 1960s, when secondary passenger services and goods services remained in the capable hands of 'Hall', 'Grange', 'Manor' and other classes of GWR parentage not graced with names. Mixed traffic locomotives of the '43xx' 2-6-0 and '28xx' 2-8-0 classes remained in service in large numbers, together with numerous tank locomotives of the 2-6-2T, 0-6-0PT and (in specific areas) 0-6-2T classes. The days of steam were, however, numbered and as further deliveries of 'Warships' led to the total dieselisation of the West of England main line and the Bristol main line, diesels began to infiltrate the services northwards from Bristol to Hereford and Shrewsbury.

In the summer of 1961 the first mixed-traffic diesel-hydraulics, the 'Hymek' (later Class 35) 1,700hp B-B locomotives were introduced. Eventually, 101 members of this class (D7000-7100) were built to replace the 'Halls' and 'Granges' and the larger tank locomotives; after introduction on cross-country inter-Regional trains, the 'Hymeks' first saw use on main line services on the South Wales main line in 1962. Like the BR Standard 'Britannias' before them, they were immediately welcomed by Cardiff crews and used on services more demanding than those for which the locomotives were originally intended.

Motive power more powerful than 'Warships' was required if West of England services were to be accelerated, and was needed to replace the 'Kings' on the Birmingham line. Late in 1961 the first of the 'Western' class (later Class 52) C-C diesel-hydraulics was delivered from Swindon, D1000 *Western Enterprise*. Like their smaller 'Warship' relations, these handsome 'Westerns' were based at Laira, but their first main allocation was to rosters that included trains from Paddington to Wolverhampton (and later beyond) to permit the speed-up of the services and allow the rapid mass withdrawal of the 'Kings'. In 1963 the 'Western' class workings were extended to include the South

Wales service, although here their introduction on the newly accelerated service was marred by axle faults that caused temporary withdrawal.

The introduction of the 'Westerns' on the Birmingham line enabled the service to be accelerated to give a journey time of less than two hours between Paddington and Birmingham, in an effort to retain the important business traffic that might otherwise have been lost to road or air while services from Euston were decelerated and reduced during preparations for 25kV electrification.

In general, however, the first half of the decade of development was marked more by deceleration than acceleration. In 1961, in an effort to reduce the operating deficit by improving stock utilisation and the service provided to such intermediate stations as Newbury, Westbury and Taunton, the West of England main line timetable was completely recast on a time-interval basis, with disastrous effects on overall timings. Even the 'Cornish Riviera Express' was required to interrupt its previously non-stop flight to Plymouth by stopping at Taunton and Exeter (at the expense of 15 minutes' additional journey time); the 'Bristolian' had 14 minutes added to its time to allow for a Bath stop and an increased load; and the 'Torbay Express' began to resemble a semi-fast by calling additionally at Reading, Westbury, Taunton and Newton Abbot. In the West Country, almost every London express was required to carry separate portions for Penzance/Plymouth and the Torbay lines, and restaurant car facilities were withdrawn west of Plymouth. The inevitable delay in attaching and detaching the portions, generally at Exeter St Davids, contributed to the overall deceleration of the services, delay that was endured by travellers until the services were recast again in 1969. Restaurant cars were not restored to Paddington-Penzance services in Cornwall until 1979, with the advent of HSTs.

It was mainly because of the introduction of the new timetable and the increased stock utilisation resulting from it that chocolate and cream livery was abandoned on named trains in 1962, when it proved impossible — as it had probably never been commercially sensible — to limit the use of train sets to one specific journey per day. Similarly, the combination of the partial loss of main line status, the loss of the excuse to paint stock in chocolate and cream, and the general British Railways policy of providing standard-interval fast services instead of limited 'crack expresses' resulted in the removal of names from almost all Western Region services, and today only the 'Cornish Riviera Express' and the 'Golden Hind' (otherwise indistinguishable from fellow HSTs) are so honoured.

Even more so than in the West Country, the new interval service on the Worcester line was decelerated by the insertion of additional stops at Evesham, Moreton-in-the-Marsh and Kingham; and the service to Oxford worsened. However, even at this nadir of passenger services, it was recognised that the new interval concept was intended as a basis from which, with new higher-powered locomotives, a faster and regular service attractive to the travelling public could be developed, and *Trains Illustrated* in October 1961 described the timetable as 'a beginning of a continuous process of acceleration and improvement'.

This forecast was correct. Gradually, throughout the decade, train speeds were increased and services improved so that a four-hour timing could be restored between Paddington and Plymouth (giving an average speed of 69.6mph as far as Taunton) in June 1965; approximately 20min could be knocked off the journey time between Paddington and Worcester at the same time, and the 105min schedule of the 'Bristolian' could be restored in the following year. By 1968 it was found possible to accelerate the 'Cornish Riviera Express' by a further 15 minutes and, in 1969, not only to reduce the Paddington-Plymouth best journey time to 3.5hr but also to introduce an hourly service between London and Exeter by providing alternate services to Plymouth/Penzance and Torbay.

By the end of the decade, therefore, it was clear that the Western Region was looking forward with confidence to the 1970s. The transition from steam to diesel had passed and, indeed, the prototype 'Warships' (D600-604) and D801 had already been withdrawn.

The accelerated services which were introduced on the Western Region between 1965 and 1969 were to be followed by other improvements, such as the introduction of air-conditioned rolling stock and higher-powered (Class 50) locomotives during the next decade, leading finally to the introduction of HST 125mph services on the main lines to Bristol, South Wales and the West Country which now provide a quality, regularity and speed of service unmatched elsewhere in the world. The foundations for the present success of the Western Region were laid during the years 1960-9. They were laid with such skill that the future of the Western Region now seems assured, a future of which the Great Western Railway, and Brunel himself, would be proud.

Dorking, Surrey — C. S. Heaps
May 1980

The 'Great Western Region'

1

At the beginning of 1960 the great majority of passenger and goods trains on the Western Region were still steam-hauled, generally by locomotives built or designed by the Great Western Railway, although the 'Kings' had already been displaced from their prime duties on the West of England main line. On 22 April 1958 the prototype diesel-hydraulic, No D600 *Active*, first hauled the up 'Cornish Riviera Express' from Penzance and, by 1960, all regular main-line expresses to the West Country were rostered to be diesel-powered. Only on summer weekends did the 'Kings' still head towards the West Country, as in August 1961 when No 6002 *King William IV* was photographed at the head of an up Plymouth express as it drifted down Wellington Bank (**1**); and when No 6018 *King Henry VI* (**2**) was photographed at Weston-super-Mare Locking Road in August 1962 after arrival with an excursion. The train is graced with the 'Bristolian' set made up of BR Mk I Standard coaches in chocolate and cream livery fitted with new B4 bogies. Elsewhere, however, reinvigorated with new double chimneys, the 'Kings' continued to provide the staple motive power on the

2

3

4

South Wales and Birmingham lines. (**3**) 'King' Class No 6020 *King Henry IV*, proudly displaying a Great Western route destination indicator is seen near Saunderton on 3 September 1959 hauling the 17.10 Paddington-Wolverhampton express. (**4**) Its sister engine, No 6021, *King Richard II*, photographed on 14 February 1961 at the head of the 'Cambrian Coast Express' on Fosse Road Bank, resplendent with smokebox headboard and hauling a matching smart rake of BR standard coaches in ex-Great Western chocolate and cream livery. By this date the ex-GWR numerical train identification number had been replaced by the new BR 4-character head code system (introduced on the Western Region at the beginning of the summer timetable in 1960) intended more easily to identify the destination and character of trains, both passenger and goods, in substitution for the traditional headlight code. Until new diesels fitted with four-panel indicators could be introduced, the new system was used on steam locomotives in conjunction with the old headlight system and No 6021 displays 'express passenger' headlamps and the letter 'A' to indicate the destination of the train as the London District (Paddington).

5

6

(**5**) No 7818 *Granville Manor* with the 'Cambrian Coast Express' near Bow Street in August 1960. To the very last days of steam, the locomotives hauling the 'Cambrian Coast Express' were kept in spotless condition on the Welsh section of the services, and the appearance of No 7818 gives no indication that its days were numbered.

Equally immaculate is the appearance of No 7022 *Hereford Castle* photographed near West Ealing on 25 August 1962 (**6**) heading a West Country express from Paddington made up of BR coaches variously painted in the then-standard maroon and recently-abandoned chocolate and cream liveries. By this time *Hereford Castle* must have been one of the last top link steam locomotives to remain allocated to Plymouth (Laira) Shed (83D). In the background, ex-WD 2-8-0 No 90225 is overtaken while travelling light engine on the slow line.

Both No 7022 and sister engine No 7027 *Thornbury Castle* were built at Swindon after nationalisation. No 7027 is seen (**7**) carrying the distinctive headboard designed for the 'Cathedrals Express', heading the up train from Hereford and Worcester through Iver (Bucks) in July 1961. With the exception of the ex-LNER Gresley-designed third coach, the sparkling set of chocolate and cream BR standard Mk 1 coaches sets off to advantage the immaculate 'Castle' at its head. The photograph epitomises the 'Great Western Region': the coaches and the

7

locomotive may have been constructed after the Great Western Railway ceased to exist, but both show how the Western Region sought, as far as possible, to ignore the fact that nationalisation had taken place.

After the abolition of the experimental blue livery applied initially to top link locomotives, it became official BR policy to paint main-line locomotives in a livery of fully-lined brunswick green, and to paint mixed-traffic locomotives, goods locomotives and tank engines in black. The official locomotive livery policy was yet another to be breached by the Western Region. As early as September 1955, the first 'Modified Hall' mixed-traffic locomotives were turned out from Swindon in express lined green livery, to be followed in due course not only by mixed-traffic locomotives of the 'Hall', 'Grange' and 'Manor' classes, but also by goods and tank engines. (**8**) Clean 'Hall' 4-6-0 No 6923 *Croxteth Hall* leaves a pall of dirty smoke over admiring holidaymakers on the sea wall at Teignmouth when hauling an up Wolverhampton express on 4 August 1962.

8

9

11

0

The express passenger livery even enhanced the appearance of the 'County' class 4-6-0s, whose lines had suffered when they received somewhat squat new double blastpipes and chimneys between 1956 and 1959. (**9**) No 1016 *County of Hants* from Shrewsbury shed (84G) enters Hereford on 29 April 1960 at the head of the 13.15 Shrewsbury-Hereford when deputising for a failed diesel multiple-unit.

Even the smallest passenger tank locomotives, the '14xx' 0-4-2T class, were adorned with express livery, as worn by No 1451, photographed on 8 August 1962 at the branch terminus at Hemyock on arrival with the 13.42 from Tiverton Junction (**10**), consisting of one milk tank and an ex-Barry Railway gas-lit coach. The full panoply of express coach livery, as well as express locomotive livery, was applied in 1956 to the Western Region's sole surviving narrow-gauge branch, the Vale of Rheidol line between Aberystwyth and Devil's Bridge. (**11**) 2-6-2T No 7 *Owain Glyndŵr* runs round its 'express passenger stock' at Aberystwyth on August Bank Holiday, 1 August 1960. The three tank locomotives on the line had been named *Owain Glyndŵr*, *Llywelyn* and *Prince of Wales* in 1956 when, following the successful restoration of the Talyllyn and the Festiniog narrow gauge railways by amateur preservationists, British Railways realised the tourist potential of its unique service. The stock on the line lost its Great Western livery after North Wales was transferred to the London Midland Region as part of the boundary reorganisations that took place on 1 January 1963 and both locomotives and stock are now decked in BR standard blue livery; nontheless since the end of the 1960s the appeal of the line, to railway enthusiasts in particular, has been enhanced by it enjoying the privilege of remaining the only steam operated section of British Railways.

The 'Great Western Region' policy that began in 1955 came to an end in 1962, after the appointment of Stanley Raymond as Regional General Manager, as was made manifest by the abolition of chocolate and cream livery during the summer of that year. The abolition took place by stealth, with the result that the public relations department at Paddington was denying any change of policy in response to enquiries from the *Western Morning News* even after new stock in maroon livery had been in use on the 'Cornish Riviera Express'.

Another sign of change was the withdrawal, for the second time, of the GWR 4-4-0 No 3440 *City of Truro*, the locomotive first credited with achieving 100mph, which had been brought out of York Museum in 1956 for use on enthusiasts' specials on the Western Region. In 1962 *City of Truro* was withdrawn from active service again and, after further restoration as No 3717, was installed as one of the major exhibits in the GWR museum opened in Swindon on 23 June 1962.

The Diesel Age Begins

The Great Western Railway had been the first of the 'Big Four' widely to use diesel traction for passenger work. The first AEC-engined railcar was introduced in 1933 and, by 1944, 38 railcars (two of which were parcel cars) were in service on the GWR. Most of these still remained in service by the beginning of the 1960s, and (**12**) 1940-built No W20W is shown at Henwick on 9 September 1961 forming the 16.10 Worcester-Bromyard service. The last ex-GWR railcar was withdrawn in 1962 but Nos 4, 20 and 22 have been preserved.

Despite its early experiments with diesel railcars, the GWR, unlike the LMSR and the Southern Railway, made no plans after the end of World War 2 to experiment with main-line diesel traction, although orders were placed for two experimental gas-turbine locomotives. The second to be delivered, the Metropolitan-Vickers/Hawksworth Co-Co design, No 18100 (introduced in 1951), was withdrawn in 1958, but the earlier Brown-Boveri Swiss-designed A1A-A1A No 18000 (introduced in 1949) remained in service at the beginning of 1960 (**13**). After initial trials on the West of England main line, it saw most service on the Paddington-Bristol route but was not renowned for its reliability. It was withdrawn in December 1960 after the prototypes of the new Western Region motive power stud — the diesel-hydraulic locomotives — had already begun to make their mark.

The first main-line diesel locomotive to be delivered to the Western Region was the North British Locomotive Company's Type 4 A1A-A1A No 600 *Active*. Sadly, its debut on the Western Region was anything but active. On a demonstration run staged on 17 February 1958 attended not only by the Chairman of the British Transport Commission but also by the Minister of Transport & Civil Aviation, one of the twin NBL/MAN 12-cylinder 1,000hp engines had to be shut down on the return journey because of a seized bearing. Despite an unbooked stop at Hullavington, the demonstration trip was not a total disaster, as the locomotive was able to return to Paddington at a speed of about 60mph running on the one remaining engine. D600 began regular service between Plymouth and Penzance at the beginning of May 1958, and as they were delivered the four other members of the class — *Ark Royal, Bulldog, Conquest* and *Cossack* — joined the prototype on service between Paddington, Plymouth and Penzance. The five A1A-A1A 'Warships' spent all their early years working on West of England main-line services. (**14**) No D601 *Ark Royal* heads the down 'Cornish Riviera Express' out of Newton Abbot on 20 February 1960. From 1962 these diesels were confined to working between Plymouth and Penzance, where they continued in service until autumn 1967 when they were briefly allocated to Cardiff (Landore) before withdrawal shortly afterwards.

The D600 class saw less and less main line service as the Swindon-built B-B 'Warships' of the D800 class (later Class 42) were introduced. The new class was a lighter design, based on German railways practice, employing two Bristol Siddeley-Maybach engines to give 2,200bhp; 38 members of the class were built (D800-832; 866-870) to be joined by 33 further similar locomotives constructed by North British, who adopted the design in preference to its earlier D600 version. D833-865 were later designated Class 43 and were almost identical to Class 42 in external appearance, although internally the North British locomotives were fitted with an uprated 1,000hp version of the NBL/MAN engines installed in *Active*.

12

13

14

The first Class 42 locomotive, D800, was named *Sir Brian Robertson*, after the Chairman of the British Transport Commission, at Paddington on 14 July 1958 and began revenue service on the down 'Cornish Riviera' on the following day.

Like the D600 class, the first 13 Class 42 locomotives were fitted with train description discs, and in (**15**) D803 *Albion* displays the traditional express passenger headcode whilst approaching Dawlish on the 10.40 Paddington-Newquay and Falmouth express on Sunday 25 June 1961. D813 *Diadem*, which was delivered to the Western Region at the end of December 1959, was the first to be fitted with the neat new standard 4-character headcode display panel, as carried by D868 *Zephyr* when photographed (**16**) hauling the down 'Cornish Riviera Express' near Dawlish Warren, also on 25 June 1961. Although the Sunday 'Cornish Riviera' does not carry the customary headboard, the smart appearance of British Railways Mk 1 coaching stock in chocolate and cream livery is evident from the photograph. In (**17**) No D858 *Valorous* is seen approaching Bristol at Bedminster Downs with the northbound 'Devonian' in September 1968.

The Great Western Railway and the Western Region had always made use of train identification numbers, particularly during periods of high traffic density, and the early 'Warships'

15

16

17

18

were designed to carry ex-GWR type painted train description numbers. Even the D600 class and the early members of Class 42 could, therefore, carry the greater part of the new 4-character headcode introduced by the Western Region — the first Region of British Railways to do so — in June 1960 — and in (**18**) the headcode discs and 'C' destination headcode indicate that No D811 *Daring* is heading an express passenger train originating within the Western Region towards the Plymouth Division.

The photograph (**18**) also epitomises the Western Region in 1962. The diesel locomotive is painted in the green livery worn by generations of Great Western steam locomotives and proudly carries an historic Great Western train name depicted on a headboard obviously originally designed for use on the smokebox of a steam locomotive. Immediately behind the engine, and elsewhere in the train, some of the coaches carry ex-GWR chocolate and cream livery but already, following the official abolition of the use of chocolate and cream, the latest BR standard Mk 1 coaches on Commonwealth bogies have been included in the train in standard maroon livery. Notwithstanding its express passenger designation, the 'Torbay Express' is pulling away from a stop at Westbury, one of a number of intermediate stops incorporated in the schedule of the 'Torbay Express' at the beginning of the winter 1961/62 timetable.

In 1962, the 'nose' of D811 had not been disfigured by the application of a yellow rectangle framing the four-character headcode panel in compliance with recommendations from the Ministry of Transport. The first locomotive to be so treated was Class 43 No D845 *Sprightly* which emerged from Swindon with its roof ends painted white and with limited yellow paint surrounding the headcode panels; it was photographed (**19**) entering Bristol Temple Meads on 26 June 1963 at the head of the 16.00 Plymouth-Liverpool. Thereafter a larger expanse of yellow paint was applied, as shown on No D830 *Majestic* seen in (**20**) heading the down 'Torbay Express' out of Paignton on 30 August 1964 over a section of line subsequently sold by British Railways to the Torbay Steam Railway. D830 was unique; it was the only member of Class 42 to be fitted with two 1,200hp Paxman Ventura engines in place of the normal 1,100hp Bristol Siddeley/Maybach units. Being the odd man out, D830 was the first non-prototype 'Warship' to be withdrawn (in 1969), only a year after D600-4 and D800-2 had reached the end of the line.

The 'Warships' were main-line express locomotives, but the West of England dieselisation scheme could not be completed without the introduction of a smaller diesel locomotive suitable for branch line and light goods work. From the same stable as *Active*, and with a clear family likeness, came the North British Locomotive Company's B-B Type 2 (later Class 22) 1,000/1,100hp diesel-hydraulic locomotives numbered in the D6300-6357 series. The first six locomotives (Nos 6300-5 were fitted with a single NBL/MAN 12-cylinder engine similar to the two engines in *Active* and her sister engines — with which they could work in multiple — but the later Type 2 locomotives were powered by the larger 1,100hp engine and could work in multiple with the later 'Warships', Nos D803-870. When first introduced, the early 1,000hp locomotives were often used in multiple hauling express trains between Plymouth and Penzance such as the 'Royal Duchy' and the 'Cornishman', and they were equally at home on main line or branch line duty. In (**21**) No 6356 is seen shunting a parcels train at Newton Abbot, while in (**22**) another member of the class fitted with 4-character destination blinds, No D6345, departs from Helston at the head of the 16.35 (SO) to Gwinear Road on 30 June 1962, four months before the withdrawal of passenger services from the branch. On this date No D6345 had been in service for less than two months, and it is perhaps ironic that many locomotives of this class should have seen early service on the Helston and the Newquay-Perranporth-Chacewater branches which were already doomed.

19

20

21

22

23

24

25

In (**23**) Class 22 No D6336 stands at the head of a goods train peeping out from the overall roof of Moretonhampstead station on 12 June 1964, two months after the official closure of the branch. On this occasion D6336 headed the last train to travel over the line between Heathfield and Moretonhampstead, when, to the surprise of local inhabitants, the daily pick-up freight from Newton Abbot to Heathfield was specially extended to the terminus for the benefit of members of the University of Exeter Railway Society. An unidentified member of the class is seen in the official photograph (**24**) of the rebuilt station at Plymouth (formerly North Road) opened by Dr Beeching on 26 March 1962.

Save for the last members of Class 22, all the 'Baby Warships' were initially allocated to Plymouth (Laira) and Newton Abbot, as were the 'Warships' in both the D600 and D800 series. Unlike the Class 22 locomotives, however, the 'Warships' of Classes 42/3 soon saw service beyond the West of England main line as, from the start, their rosters included workings between Taunton and Bristol, and between Bristol and Paddington. Classes 42/3 saw early service on south-west-north-west workings north of Bristol, and newly delivered Class 43 No D833 *Panther* was photographed (**25**) near Hereford hauling the 09.10 Liverpool-Plymouth on 1 May 1962. In the following year, on 22 June 1963, No D817 *Foxhound*, was seen entering Hereford station — passing station pilot 'Modified Hall' No 7906 *Fron Hall* — at the head of a Manchester-bound service from the south-west (**26**). Later Class 47s saw service on the line through Pontypool Road,

26

27

where Nos D1734 and D1750 were photographed on 26 August 1964 (**27**).

On the ex-Midland main line between Bristol and Gloucester, for which the WR had gained responsibility in 1958, 'Peaks' (later Class 45) were introduced early in the decade, as shown in (**28**) by an unidentified but clearly new member of this class photographed at Norton Crossing (near Worcester) at the head of the southbound 'Pines Express' on 14 April 1962. This section north of Bristol included the notorious Lickey incline, up which many trains required banking assistance. The Western Region first provided 0-6-0PTs and Class 9F 2-10-0s as bankers, but later Class 37 diesel-electric locomotives took over this task, as on 16 August 1966 when No D6941 assisted D19 up the incline on an up train from Bristol (**29**).

28

29

30

Bristol and South Wales

Although by 1960 the majority of main-line expresses between Paddington and Plymouth (via the Berks & Hants line) were diesel-hauled, most trains heading west from Reading to Swindon and thence to Bristol and South Wales were still hauled by steam locomotives. On the South Wales expresses, BR Standard 4-6-2 'Britannia' locomotives still reigned supreme and (**30**) shows No 70022 *Tornado* passing Westbourne Park at the head of the 13.55 from Paddington to West Wales on 18 April 1960. The first 'Britannias' to be allocated to the Western Region, in 1952, had been placed in service between Plymouth and Penzance. Despite being the first Pacific locomotives to work on the Western Region in Devon and Cornwall, they were not welcomed by Great Western diehards in the south-west and were not totally accepted on the Western Region until all members of the class were transferred to Cardiff Canton for use on the South Wales expresses, after which they were regularly rostered for use on the 'Capitals United Express' and the 'Red Dragon'. Deliveries of 'Warships' to the West of England main line, however, released 'Kings' for main-line duty elsewhere on the Western Region and in mid-1960 six 'King' class 4-6-0s, Nos 6003/4/18/19/23/28, were allocated to Cardiff Canton. This transfer enabled the Western Region 'Britannias' to be transferred to the London Midland Region, although retaining their historic ex-GWR names (eg *Morning Star, Western Star*) and the modified smoke deflectors introduced after the first fatal accident on the Western Region in November 1955. It was claimed on that occasion that the handrails on the 'Britannia's' smoke deflectors had contributed to the derailment of No 70026 *Polar Star* at Milton on 20 November 1955; the handrails evident in the photograph of the stricken No 70026 in (**31**) were replaced by the recessed handholds that are conspicuous on No 70022 in (**30**).

The BR Standard Pacifics were transferred from the Western Region only months after Swindon Works completed the construction of the last steam locomotive for British Railways, Class 9F 2-10-0 No 92220 *Evening Star*.

Alone among the 251 heavy goods locomotives of its class, *Evening Star* was accorded the honour of a name when unveiled at Swindon on 18 March 1960 by Mr K. W. C. Grand, the last Assistant General Manager of the GWR and then a Member of the British Transport Commission. The locomotive (**32**) was turned out in fully lined express passenger green livery and 'Great Westernised' by the use of a copper-capped chimney. Alone among BR Standard classes, Class 9F won total acceptance by Western Region drivers, with the result that they were used not only on the heavy goods traffic for which they were intended but also, on occasion, on express passenger duty including, until banned by higher authority, the 'Capitals United

31

70026

32

THE LAST STEAM LOCOMOTIVE TO BE BUILT
"EVENING STAR"
BUILT IN SWINDON WORKS AND NAMED ON MARCH
EVENING STAR

33

34

Express' in late June and early July 1960. In (**33**) Class 9F No 92206 stands at the buffer stops at Paddington after arrival with an up Bristol or South Wales express, whilst in (**34**) No 92209 coasts through Patchway with an up empty stock train on 10 August 1963.

Three years earlier, on 24 May 1960, No 92237 was seen passing Oldfield Park, Bath (**35**) on the heavy goods duty for which the class was originally designed, although No 92006, photographed passing Bridgend on 7 July 1962 (**36**) should not have been severely taxed by the weight of its train.

35

36

37

Express steam on the Bristol main line is represented by (**37**) which shows 'Castle' class 4-6-0 No 7014 *Caerhays Castle* piloting 'King' No 6015 *King Richard III* near Didcot at the head of the 07.00 Weston-super-Mare-Paddington express on Monday 23 May 1960. This was a regular double-headed turn on Mondays at the time. 'Castle' No 5078 *Beaufort* required no assistance as it accelerated away from a signal stop at Southall at the head of the down 'Pembroke Coast Express' on 23 December 1961 (**38**). Although the bulk of the train is made up of BR Standard coaches in chocolate and cream livery, this formation amply demonstrates the mixed liveries to be seen on the Western Region at this time as the train includes (immediately behind the locomotive) an ex-GWR coach in the former standard 'raspberry and cream' livery followed by two coaches painted maroon. Green-painted *Beaufort* makes a fine sight at its head, complete with silver-painted buffers and sparkling paintwork, in marked contrast to the run-down appearance of 'Hall' class No 4968 *Shotton Hall* seen in (**39**) leaving the gloom of the overall roof at Bristol Temple Meads on 10 August 1961 at the head of the 'Cities of Bristol and Bath' holiday express to Bournemouth.

38

39

40

Steadily, throughout 1960 and 1961, the increasing numbers of 'Warship' diesel-hydraulics led to the replacement of steam power on most London-Bristol expresses, and in (**40**) the headcode 1B08 on No D856 *Trojan* indicates the Bristol destination of its down express photographed near Slough. In (**41**) No D851 *Temeraire* passes Scours Lane Sidings, Reading, at the head of the 11.35 Weston-super-Mare-Paddington on 17 October 1964, the leading coach of which carries a Continental style coach destination board of a design introduced experimentally by the Western Region in the early 1960s. Although no doubt easier to manipulate than the old style long boards traditionally fixed above the carriage windows, which can clearly be seen in (**6**) and (**18**), the experiment was not a success and was later discontinued. Today the practice of coach destination marking has been dropped by British Railways because of the frequent changes that would be necessary with present complicated rolling stock workings.

At the beginning of the 1960s the 'South Wales Pullman' (introduced in 1955) was still 'Castle'-hauled on its daily journey from Paddington to Swansea and back here (**42**) by No 5016 *Montgomery Castle* on 28 April 1959 — but in 1961 the Western Region invested in three eight-car 'Blue Pullman' sets and allocated one set to the South Wales service. On the introduction of the new timetable in September 1961 a second set was allocated to a new 'Bristol Pullman' and the South Wales service was revised to run up in the morning and return in the evening. Both Pullmans were timed to arrive in London so as to enable businessmen from Bristol and South Wales to enjoy air-conditioned comfort on their day trips to the capital. Although mid-day trips from Paddington to Bristol and back (and also to Oxford and back for a short period in 1967) attracted little patronage, the morning and evening 'Bristol Pullmans' were sufficiently popular to justify the units being used in multiple when spare sets became available after the withdrawal of the 'Birmingham Pullman' in 1967. In (**43**) the down evening 'Bristol Pullman' was photographed near Iver on 8 June 1962;

41

42

43

44

by 21 August 1969, when the 'South Wales Pullman' (**44**) was captured approaching Paddington at Subway Junction, the new BR Pullman livery had been applied.

The two liveries are easily compared in the photograph (**45**) of the down 'South Wales Pullman' seen near Pangbourne on 10 October 1968.

The rosters for the 'Warships' based at Plymouth did not include the South Wales services, and these services remained steam hauled until the introduction of the Type 3 (later Class 35) Beyer Peacock (Hymek) 1,700hp B-B diesel-hydraulics, of which the first was delivered in May 1961. They were immediately given responsibility for the South Wales-Paddington services on which they commenced replacing 'Kings' and 'Castles' in spring 1962. In (**46**), before the abolition of chocolate and cream livery, No D7022 slows to make an unscheduled stop at Badminton on 13 April 1962 with the up 'Red Dragon' whilst on the following day, D7023 is seen in (**47**) calling at Reading General at the head of the 09.00 Cardiff-Paddington. The inclusion of a chocolate and cream second class coach at the front of this train, and the insertion of a maroon coach in the 'Red Dragon', well illustrates the difficulties faced by Western Region authorities in endeavouring to distinguish named train and 'other' passenger coach workings. Badminton station is another example of change during the decade of development. It was closed to passenger traffic on 3 June 1968, but only after British Railways had obtained powers by Act of Parliament to abrogate the rights enjoyed by the Duke of Beaufort to require a minimum of trains each day to call at the station.

45

46

47

48

'Hymeks' also saw early service on cross-country trains between Bristol and West Wales, and Bristol and Portsmouth. They were modern substitutes for mixed traffic locomotives such as 'Grange' and 'Hall' 4-6-0s, an example of which, No 4967 *Shirenewton Hall*, is seen in (**48**) entering Bridgend station with a Swansea-Weston-super-Mare excursion on 7 July 1962. The modern, clean lines of the Class 35s, one of the earliest classes to benefit from advice from the BR Design Panel, are clearly seen in the photographs of Nos D7024 and D7014 at Cardiff General on 7 July 1962 and 20 August 1963 respectively (**49**) (**50**).

The 'Hymeks' did not see extensive service on the West of England main line, although it was not uncommon for them to be used on summer services. In (**51**), one of the early members of the class No D7006 (still devoid of yellow warning panel) heads an up express to Wolverhampton along the seawall at Teignmouth on 4 August 1962. The coaches towards the rear of the Wolverhampton express are of pre-nationalisation design, as are all the coaches forming the Weston-super-Mare excursion illustrated in (**48**).

49

50

51

52

A considerable number of non-standard coaches constructed prior to nationalisation — and even a few coaches prior to the Grouping in 1923 — remained in service at the beginning of 1960 for use particularly on excursions, and in his report published in 1963 Dr Beeching commented unfavourably upon the retention of such reserve coaching stock which was 'expensive to supply, maintain, and assemble' and which was idle for most of the year. In the report he pointed out that 2,000 coaches were used on not more than ten occasions a year, and 6,000 coaches were in traffic not more than 18 times. He estimated that the annual cost of providing the 6,000 coaches was £3.4million but that they only contributed net income of £0.5million to railway revenue. Following implementation of his report, the great majority of non-standard locomotive-hauled coaches were steadily but speedily withdrawn. A particularly 'vintage' collection of non-standard coaches is illustrated in (**52**) forming the 'Cambrian Radio Cruise' leaving Barmouth bridge on 24 July 1961 hauled by BR Standard Class 4 4-6-0 No 75034.

Although the 'Warships' in Bristol and the 'Hymeks' at Cardiff and Swansea were the first main line diesel locomotives to break the monopoly of steam power, some local passenger services had succumbed in the late 1950s to diesel multiple-units. Many of the minor branch lines, which were to be closed under the Beeching proposals, remained steam operated, among them the Pontardulais-Llandeilo service on which 0-6-0PT No 9621 was photographed at Ffairfach Halt on 4 September, 1963 (**53**). This line still retains a passenger service, albeit heavily subsidised, as part of the Central Wales line between Swansea and Shrewsbury, for the closure of which permission has been refused for social (and no doubt political) reasons on more than one occasion. Even though a Minister of Transport once claimed that it would have been cheaper to supply all passengers on the line with individual motor cars rather than to run the service, the conversion of the Central Wales line to a 'basic railway' using the minimum possible level of staff and signalling, and imaginative publicity have resulted in increased use of the line and its retention as an important link in local communications.

Although the main part of the Central Wales line was reprieved, Ministry consent for closure was granted in respect of the ex-LNWR section from Swansea Victoria to Pontardulais, on which section Standard Class 5 4-6-0 No 73092 is seen in (**54**), leaving Swansea Bay station in the direction of Swansea Victoria on 19 December 1960. In (**55**) ex-LMSR Class 5 4-6-0

53

54

SENIOR SERVICE
CIGARETTES
GIFTS
NOVELTIES
WILLS' WOODBINES

55

56

57

No 45406 leaves Swansea Victoria on 13 June 1964 at the head of the last booked train to leave the terminus, the 18.25 Swansea Victoria-York.

The passengers on the branch line between Tondu and Porthcawl lost their passenger service in the previous year, on 9 September 1963. In (**56**) push-pull fitted 0-6-OPT No 6431 was photographed at Tondu forming a three-coach auto-set for the Porthcawl branch a little over a year earlier, on 7 July 1962.

Auto-trains were used quite extensively on South Wales branches before dieselisation on minor lines, and a one-coach auto-train is seen in (**57**) at Llwydcoed on a service between Hirwaun and Merthyr propelled by 0-6-OPT No 6433 on 12 August 1961. The numerous staff to be seen on the train and on the platform, and the evidence of full signalling on the line, indicate the high cost of running the low capacity service (which enjoyed approximately six trains each way in the summer 1962 timetable), and the line closed on 31 December of that year.

On busier lines, larger locomotives were required and the standard workhorse in South Wales was the '56xx' class 0-6-2T introduced by C. B. Collett in 1924 closely following the design of earlier Welsh railway designs, 200 locomotives were constructed in the class (Nos 5600-5699, 6600-6699) and the bulk of the class spent all their days in use in South Wales on both passenger and goods work. In (**58**) No 5617 approaches Radyr with a return football excursion from Ninian Park Halt, Cardiff; and in (**59**) No 6641 was photographed at Crumlin High Level heading a service for Neath on 24 April 1961. Crumlin High Level closed on 15 June 1964 when services ceased over the lofty Crumlin Viaduct which carried the ex-Newport Abergavenny & Hereford Railway 200ft above the valley floor of Ebbw Vale.

58

59

The '56xx' class locomotives were graced, during the period of the 'Great Western Region', with express passenger green livery, as worn by No 6643 (**60**) when heading an enthusiasts' special up the 1 in 35 gradient near Cwm Bargoed on 31 July 1965. By this date, a yellow line had been applied at roof level to the leading brake composite coach to indicate the location of first class seating. Interestingly, the enthusiasts' train includes not only an ex-GWR Hawksworth coach but also one of the ex-Southern Railway Bulleid coaches that were transferred from the Southern Region (and subsequently repainted in maroon livery) for temporary use elsewhere on British Railways.

By the beginning of 1960, however, the majority of suburban passenger services in South Wales were probably provided by diesel multiple-units. Diesel railcar services were introduced in the Cardiff Valleys on 13 January 1958, and later that year, were extended to the Rhymney section. In (**61**) a 3-car Derby-built suburban unit adorned with the 'V' markings with which early multiple-units were painted, calls at Heath Halt (High Level) in the suburbs of Cardiff, forming the 13.51 Caerphilly to Cardiff (Bute Road) service on 19 August 1963; whilst in (**62**) two similar 3-car units are seen approaching Merthyr Vale on 11 August 1961 on an afternoon Merthyr-Barry Island service.

Neither the popularity of the new diesel units nor their cheaper operating costs was sufficient to avoid major passenger service withdrawals in South Wales, and on 30 April 1962 passenger services were withdrawn from the Eastern and Western Valleys in Monmouthshire between Newport and Blaenavon Low Level (with branch workings between Panteg, Pontypool Road and Abergavenny); and from Newport to Brynmawr, with branch workings from Aberbeeg to Ebbw Vale Low Level. Discontinuance of these services resulted in the closure of no fewer than 37 stations, but worse was to follow, and during the remainder of the 1960s passenger services were withdrawn from further lines in South Wales including those to Aberdare (1964), Dowlais (1962/4) New Tredegar (1962) and Blaenavon (1962).

In addition to these Valley lines, the more countrified lines to

60

61

62

63

64

65

the west of Cardiff did not remain unscathed; the few passengers seen alighting from the 12.45 Cardiff (Clarence Road) to Pontypridd via St Fagins at Creigiau on 14 May 1962 (**63**) were only to enjoy such services for another four months. Services on the Vale of Glamorgan line lasted until June 1964; in (**64**) a smart 3-car Derby Suburban unit was photographed between Rhoose and Aberthaw on 2 July 1960. Only the services from Cardiff to Barry, and from Cardiff to Rhymney, Pontypridd, Merthyr and Treherbert managed to survive the decade, and they continue to provide an important link in South Wales communications as well as being feeder lines for the HST services from the capital of the Principality to London. The little-used (seasonal only) extension to Barry Pier only survived until 1971. The causeway to Barry Island is seen in the background of (**65**), showing 2-6-2T No 5162 approaching Barry Town with the 18.35 Barry Island-Treherbert on 7 May 1955, but Barry Island remains probably as popular with visitors and excursionists as it was in 1957 when 'Grange' 4-6-0 No 6823 *Oakley Grange* was photographed (**66**) with a Newport-Barry Island special passing Barry Dock.

66

67

69

The '56xx' 0-6-2T locomotives were used as much on goods duties as on passenger work. In (**67**) No 5635 passes Cherry Orchard Wagon Works on 19 August 1963 hauling a train of empty wagons, while in (**68**) green-liveried No 6688 restarts an empty iron-ore train away from Taffs Wells past Pentyrch Crossing towards Cardiff on 17 February 1962. The supremacy of the '56xx' class was soon to be challenged by the first diesel-electric (as opposed to diesel-hydraulic) main line locomotives to be introduced on the Western Region, the English Electric Type 3 locomotives in the D6700 series (later Class 37). Delivery of new locomotives to Cardiff Canton began in April 1963 when they saw early service on the shuttle service of iron ore trains between Newport Docks and the steelworks at Llanwern. These trains were instituted after the opening of the steelworks by the Queen on 26 October 1962 and were originally worked on a Push-Pull basis by ex-GWR 2-8-0Ts of the '42xx' class. In (**69**) Type 3 B-B diesel-electric No D6820 stands at Ffaldcaiach signalbox Llancaiach, awaiting banking

68

70

9H28

71

5T17
THE 300TH
ENGLISH ELECTRIC
STANDARD TYPE 3 DIESEL ELECTRIC LOCOMOTIVE
FOR BRITISH RAILWAYS

72

assistance from 0-6-2T No 5621, of the class being displaced by the new diesels. In (**70**) No D6819 heads a down coal train on the former Taff Railway Roath branch on 17 August 1963 and in (**71**) D6999 — on its first revenue-earning service — heads a block coal train to Spencer Steel Works at Llanwern on 12 October 1965. These English Electric locomotives rapidly took over most freight working in South Wales, replacing not only the 0-6-2T classes but also the larger 2-8-0T and 2-8-2T large mineral tanks, the Churchward 2-8-0 goods locomotives and even the small but powerful 0-6-0PT classes. In (**72**) 2-8-2T No 7203 emerges from High Street Tunnel, Newport, with a train of empties for the Western Valley on 2 March 1961; in (**73**)

73

74

2-8-0 No 3801 comes off the Bishton flyover (near Magor) which was built to carry freight trains direct from Llanwern Steel Works to Severn Tunnel Junction; and in (**74**) 0-6-0PT No 9482 passes the site of the Llanwern Steel Works (construction can be seen in progress on the right) on 9 June 1960. In (**75**) Class 57xx 0-6-0PT No 3785 double-heads Class 94xx 0-6-0PT No 9484 near Swansea at the head of a freight for West Wales on 21 June 1961.

75

76

77

Changes on the Birmingham Line

The introduction of 'Warships' on the West of England main line at the end of the 1950s led to the transfer of the 'King' 4-6-0s from West Country duties to service on the South Wales main line and the ex-GWR Birmingham main line from Paddington via Banbury and Leamington Spa. At the beginning of 1960, the Birmingham trains were in the capable hands of 'Kings', and in (**76**) an immaculate 'King' No 6017 *King Edward IV* is seen at the head of the 14.10 Paddington-Birkenhead train passing Park Royal on 4 August 1960. Birkenhead being part of the London Midland Region, the locomotive carries the headcode 'M02' indicating that the destination of the train is on the Midland Region, whilst in (**77**) the chalked headcode 'A10' carried by No 6016 *King Edward V* indicates that the destination of the up 'Cambrian Coast Express' is Paddington. No 6016 was photographed in Saunderton cutting between Princes Risborough and High Wycombe, where for a short distance the up and down line of the ex-Great Western & Great Central joint line were constructed in separate cuttings. The year 1960 saw the end of a feature of railway practice that had been unique to the Great Western Railway and the Western Region since shortly before World War 2 — the slip coach. Slip coach working, which had surprisingly been re-introduced after the end of the war, slowly diminished during the 1950s when (for example) the slip for Westbury off the down 'Cornish Riviera Express' (for which reasonably modern Hawksworth coaches were re-equipped and repainted in chocolate and cream livery in 1956) was withdrawn, but the last working survived into 1960

78

79

80

to provide a service to Bicester North from Paddington on the 17.10 Paddington-Wolverhampton. In (**78**) 'Hall' class 4-6-0 No 4907 *Broughton Hall* has collected the slip coach W7071W — which can be recognised by the double tail lights — from the down main line and is preparing to attach the coach to proceed as part of the 16.34 Paddington-Wolverhampton semi-fast on 31 May 1960. This slip working, the last on British Railways, ceased not long after, on 9 September of that year, when no fewer than four coaches were required on the slip portion.

The ex-GWR main line from Paddington to Birmingham was to enjoy an Indian summer during the early 1960s. It was inevitable that services on the ex-LNWR main line from Euston to Birmingham would need to be greatly decelerated and reduced when a major works scheme on the 25V electrification began in earnest in 1962. Particularly as Birmingham already enjoyed the benefit of the M1 Motorway, British Railways thought it important to maintain business traffic by providing an alternative fast service from the capital to Birmingham on the ex-GWR line and, in the 1962 winter timetable, the Western Region Birmingham trains were accelerated substantially to provide at least eight services in each direction between Paddington and Birmingham (Snow Hill) on 2-hour timings. This acceleration would not have been possible using the ageing 'Kings', but at the end of 1961 the first of the Type 4 C-C 2,700hp diesel-hydraulic 'Western' class locomotives was delivered, D1000 *Western Enterprise*. These locomotives (later Class 52,) although shedded at Plymouth (Laira), were first put to work on the Paddington-Birmingham service and in (**79**) the prototype No D1000 — painted in an experimental 'desert sand' livery — pauses at Birmingham Snow Hill to collect an encouragingly large number of London-bound businessmen. On the platform can be seen notices advertising two other services introduced for the benefit of Midlands businessmen, the BR/BEA connecting bus service from High Wycombe to London Airport (Heathrow) and the 'Birmingham Pullman' air-conditioned service which was introduced on 12 September 1960. The down 'Birmingham Pullman' (16.50 from Paddington) is seen in (**80**) approaching High Wycombe on 20 August 1965 in its original livery. Not long after, the Pullman Company coat of arms below the driver's windows was obliterated by the inevitable yellow warning panel, whilst towards the end of the 1960s all the Western Region Pullman units were repainted in the new 'Pullman style' of grey and blue first adopted on the introduction of the Manchester and Liverpool Pullmans upon completion of the Midland Region electrification from Euston.

81

82

83

When the 'Birmingham Pullman' and 'Bristol Pullman' were originally introduced in 1960, a spare Pullman set was kept in reserve. This uneconomic measure for guaranteeing air-conditioned comfort for Pullman passengers was abandoned in the following year, when the spare set was used on the 'South Wales Pullman,' and thereafter a set of locomotive-hauled traditional Pullmans was maintained as a 'stand-by' train. In (**81**) maroon painted 'Western' No D1006 *Western Stalwart* is seen passing Princes Risborough at the head of the down 'Birmingham Pullman' on 12 July 1962, the standby coaching set being made up of five traditional Pullman cars augmented by two British Railways standard open firsts painted in umber and cream to match the Pullman cars.

Before the introduction of the all-embracing blue livery adopted by British Railways, the 'Westerns' appeared in several liveries including 'desert sand', maroon, green and golden ochre. The first two 'Westerns' constructed at Swindon, Nos D1000/1, were turned out in 'desert sand' and green livery respectively; D1002/3/4 were painted green at Swindon but thereafter Swindon delivered its 'Westerns' painted in maroon livery. Meanwhile, Crewe Works delivered its first four 'Westerns' (D1035-8) in green livery, before also adopting the standard maroon livery used for 'Western' and 'Warship' locomotives. In (**82**) the first Crewe-built 'Western,' No D1035 *Western Yeoman* was photographed on 18 October 1962 approaching High Wycombe at the head of the 11.40 Birkenhead-Paddington express.

Like the 'Hymeks,' the 'Westerns' also enjoyed the benefit of advice from the BR Design Panel, and the clean lines of the class can be clearly seen in the photograph of No D1010 *Western Campaigner* passing Leamington Spa General when almost new at the head of a down Birkenhead express (**83**).

84

The 'Westerns' delivered in 1962 were only sufficient to take over the main Birmingham expresses, and steam power continued to be used on many semi-fasts, inter-Regional and goods trains for some years. In (**84**) 'Modified Hall' class No 6971 *Athelhampton Hall* was photographed passing Hatton station with an up freight on 29 September 1962, about to meet sister locomotive No 6991 *Acton Burnell Hall* (**85**). Meanwhile, 'Castle' 4-6-0s continued to power passenger trains other than the two-hour expresses. In (**86**) a spotless double-chimney 'Castle', No 5088 *Llanthony Abbey* approaches Old Oak with a football excursion from the Birmingham area, passing a 3-car Pressed Steel surburban diesel multiple-unit on a service to Uxbridge (a passenger service withdrawn in

85

86

87

September 1962); whilst in (**87**) 'Castle' No 5068 *Beverston Castle* picks up water from Aynho Troughs while hauling the 11.05 Wolverhampton-Bournemouth on 19 May 1962. Also taking up water from troughs, this time at Ruislip, is 'Castle' 4-6-0 No 5008 *Raglan Castle* (**88**) as it heads the 18.10 Paddington-Shrewsbury express on Sunday, 2 September 1962. Only a few years later, the withdrawal of steam from British Railways sounded the death knell for water troughs, which had served the steam locomotive well for over 100 years.

The Birmingham line was only served by 'Westerns' for a period of two or three years. By the end of 1962 the British Railways Board had resolved that its long term future lay with diesel-electric locomotives and not with diesel-hydraulics, and the introduction of English Electric Type 3 diesel-electrics in South Wales in 1962 was followed by the introduction of Brush Type 4 Co-Co (later Class 47) diesel-electrics on the Paddington-West Midlands services in 1964. The locomotives started passenger work in January of that year, and the spotless external appearance of No D1714 (**89**) seen on arrival at Paddington with the 14.35 train from Birkenhead on 7 April 1964 clearly shows that the locomotive has not long been in service. Some months later, even the pleasing two-tone livery of sister locomotive No D1715 — seen heading the 7.40 Birkenhead-Paddington train near West Wycombe on 26 September 1964 (**90**) — cannot hide the fact that the locomotive has been in service for some months.

88

89

90

91

Accelerated Services to Wales and the South-West

Continuing deliveries of the 'Westerns', of which 74 were eventually built, and their release from London-Birmingham services enabled the Western Region to accelerate services from Paddington to South Wales and the West of England.

Before their introduction on the Paddington-Birmingham route, the early members of the class saw service on the West of England main line working on D800 Type 4 diagrams, but after their introduction to Birmingham services on 25 June 1962 their use on West of England services was limited, in early years, to services forming part of rosters taking them to and from their Plymouth (Laira) home base to West Midlands workings. No 1023 *Western Fusilier* was photographed in (**91**) climbing Dainton Bank at the head of the 09.20 Paddington-Penzance relief on 12 April 1974. The 'Westerns' were permitted to haul 525 tons unassisted over the South Devon banks on the then existing diesel timings, as against 380 tons for a D600 and 400 tons for a D800 class on passenger working. In (**92**) D1003 *Western Pioneer* was photographed at Savernake Low Level on 1 September 1962 on an up West of England express.

The first signs of a speed-up to the West came in 1964. Anxious to increase the morale both of passengers and employees in the south-west in the wake of the Beeching recommendations, the Plymouth Divisional Manager, Mr David Pattisson, proposed a new high speed businessman's train from Plymouth to Paddington that was to be introduced as the 'Golden Hind' on 15 June 1964. The feasibility of the proposed timings was put to the test on 8 April of that year, when a high-speed proving run was carried out between Paddington and Plymouth. A seven-coach train, including track recording coach, hauled by No D1027 *Western Lancer* — seen in (**93**) approaching Teignmouth — was scheduled to reach Plymouth in 200min. Although permanent way repairs, and possibly cautious driving, resulted in the trip taking 208min 36sec for the 225.55 miles, this was still the fastest run in history between Paddington and Plymouth and this experimental trip (and the return journey in 203min 1sec) proved the feasibility of the proposed new service. The 'Golden Hind' was introduced with a scheduled time of 230min in the up direction (and 235min in the down direction) and, with connections from Cornwall and Exmouth, enabled West Country passengers to arrive at Paddington as early as 10.55.

Twelve days after the experimental run to Plymouth, a run took place between Bristol and Paddington to test the minimum practical time for a 'Western' on a high-speed service between Bristol and Paddington (via Bath), during which No D1023 *Western Fusilier* whisked its seven-coach train over the 118.35 miles at an average speed of 74.5mph.

These fast runs compared interestingly with a high-speed steam-hauled enthusiasts' special between Paddington and Plymouth that took place on 9 May 1964 to celebrate the 60th Anniversary of the 'Ocean Mail' run of 1904 when *City of Truro* achieved fame and honour with its long-claimed 102mph sprint down Wellington Bank.

On the down run of the enthusiasts' special, 40-year old 'Castle' No 4078 *Pendennis Castle* was exceeding the maximum speed achieved by D 1027 on the April test run when, travelling at 95/96mph near Lavington, the collapse of the firebars rapidly terminated this high-speed dash. After replacement of *Pendennis Castle* by 'Hall' No 6999 *Capel Dewi Hall* as far as

92

93

94

95

Taunton, 'Castle' No 7025 *Sudeley Castle* enthusiastically continued to Plymouth (North Road), whilst on the return journey to Paddington (via Bristol) double-chimney 'Castle' No 7029 *Clun Castle* (now preserved) achieved a maximum speed of 94mph on the bank at Wellington. Despite the disappointments surrounding the failure of *Pendennis Castle*, the trip was considered by all to be a great success and a credit to the Western Region staff concerned. As Cecil J. Allen commented in his article in *Railway World* shortly afterwards, the 'Castles' were going out in a blaze of glory. In (**94**) No 4079 *Pendennis Castle* was photographed shortly after passing Reading West on the first leg of the journey.

If the *Railway World* excursion was exciting but fun, the high-speed experimental run to Plymouth in April and the introduction of the 'Golden Hind' in June provided solid evidence of the Western Region's desire to improve express passenger timings after the nadir of 1962.

From the beginning of the winter 1962/3 timetable, the introduction of 'Westerns' on the South Wales service permitted an acceleration which was described at the time in *Modern Railways* as 'one of the most revolutionary of any that has been achieved at one stroke in Great Britain as the result of the substitution of diesel for steam power'. For the loss of through workings between Paddington and West Wales, to obtain the maximum use of rolling stock, the Principality gained a regular-interval service accelerated by up to 30min, although the prestige of this new service was somewhat dented when the 'Westerns' had to be withdrawn within a month (after the derailment of No D1000 on a Penzance parcel train had revealed roller bearing problems) to be temporarily replaced by the lower-powered 'Hymeks'. This setback was, however, only temporary, and even faster schedules were introduced between Paddington and South Wales at the beginning of the summer timetable in 1965.

On the West of England main line also, accelerations were proposed. Baulked in his desire to test a 'Deltic' on the Western Region, the General Manager, G. F. Fiennes, broke yet again the record for the journey between Paddington and Plymouth when on 3 June 1965 he experimented with a test train double-headed by English Electric Type 3 (later Class 37) Nos D6881/2, which had been regeared for higher speed. Hauling nine coaches of the experimental XP64 coaching set and a track recording car, the duo reached Plymouth (including a stop at Exeter) in 196.5min and on the return journey via Bristol covered the 118 miles from Bristol to Paddington in 87min. Subsequently, Fiennes was authorised to convert further members of the class (D 6875-92) which enabled the Western Region to introduce new high-speed schedules on 18 April 1966 employing pairs of such locomotives in multiple. Two special train sets were prepared, one the XP64 prototype train set and one a 370-ton set of coaching stock on Commonwealth bogies repainted throughout in the new blue and grey livery. These trains were permitted to run at 100mph and the new timings included an average of 75.9mph between Paddington and Bath on the 12.45 Paddington-Bristol; an average of 69.5mph from Newport to Paddington on the 08.20 Swansea-Paddington; and an average of 78.3mph between Paddington and Chippenham on the 14.45 service. The 78.3mph average between Paddington and Chippenham was then the fastest start-stop average ever known in Western Region or GWR history. The 12.45 Paddington to Bristol is seen in (**95**) at Bath Spa headed by Class 37 Nos D6882 and D6881 on 15 May 1966.

Multiple use of Class 37s continued only for a relatively short time, to be replaced in due course by single 'Westerns'. The 'Golden Hind' and Class 37 trials were followed in 1966 by the running of the first-ever non-stop passenger train between Paddington and Penzance, when Ian Allan Limited organised a special train on 7 May 1966 headed by No D1010 *Western Campaigner* which was photographed (**96**) passing Newbury on the down journey.

96

97

A 'Western' on excursion duty was photographed in (**97**) when No D1047 *Western Lord* approached Worle Junction at the head of an excursion to Weston-super-Mare, the 'special' or 'excursion' nature of the train being indicated by the 'Z' headcode.

'Westerns' also superseded 'Warships' slowly on the passenger and goods SW-NE services north of Bristol, and in (**98**) an unidentified but smart 'Western' is framed by the neat stonework of an overbridge near Lydney on a down freight.

98

99

Cheltenham-Gloucester and Worcester

The distinction of being the fastest train in the world was enjoyed for a time before World War 2 by the 'Cheltenham Flyer', whose exploits between Swindon and Paddington received world-wide acclaim. Since World War 2, however, the people of Cheltenham have received less consideration from the railway authorities and the ex-GWR main lines from Paddington to Gloucester and Cheltenham (via Swindon), and from Paddington to Worcester and Hereford (via Oxford), have not enjoyed the attention given to other parts of the Western Region. Even before the great 1961 timetable revolution, services on the Worcester line were slower than before World War 1, and in the winter 1961 timetable a further 10min was added to overall times. Neither the Worcester nor the Cheltenham services featured in the early phases of the Western Region dieselisation programme and it was on these lines that the 'Castle' class locomotives enjoyed their final fling. The 'Cheltenham Spa Express' could not be considered the true successor of the 'Cheltenham Flyer' as it did not enjoy a particularly fast timing between Cheltenham, Gloucester and Paddington, but it did, at least, give the Western Region a further excuse for the reintroduction of chocolate and cream rolling stock in 1956. In (**99**) 'Castle' No 7035 *Ogmore Castle* passes Tramway Junction on the outskirts of Gloucester at the head of the up 'Cheltenham Spa Express' in August 1960. Over two years later, the same locomotive was photographed, on 19 October 1962, leaving Sapperton Tunnel at the head of the 11.45 Paddington-Cheltenham express (**100**). In general, the 'Castles' used on the Cheltenham expresses in the last years of

00

10

10

)3

steam were kept in spotless condition, and in (**101**) No 7034 *Ince Castle* sparkles in the sunlight at the head of a clean matching rake of BR standard coaches as it climbs Sapperton Bank unassisted at the head of the 11.45 Cheltenham Spa (St James)-Paddington on 31 March 1962.

The section of line between Gloucester and Chalford enjoyed, in addition to main line trains, a regular auto-train service which survived until November 1964, when it fell victim to the Beeching Axe. In (**102**) auto-coach number W242W is seen being propelled into Brimscombe by Class 14xx 0-4-2T No 1472 towards the end of October 1964.

Another interesting mixture of main line and branch line practice was a regular feature of the services between Gloucester and Cheltenham. Services from Paddington called at Gloucester Central, where through trains to Cheltenham had to reverse, and not at the ex-LMSR station, Gloucester Eastgate. For the short eight-mile journey thence to Cheltenham, main line expresses were hauled by pannier or Prairie tank engines. In (**103**) green-liveried 2-6-2T No 4564, recently transferred from Penzance shed following dieselisation in Cornwall, heads the Cheltenham portion of a Paddington express through Lansdown Junction in July 1964.

By 1964 the end of steam on the Western Region was fast approaching and its sad decline in the Gloucester area is epitomised by (**104**) which illustrates two obviously uncared-for and unkempt locomotives, 0-6-0PT No 3775 and 'Castle' 4-6-0 No 5042 *Winchester Castle* at Gloucester Central on 3 October 1964. Earlier in the year, the shape of things to come on the Paddington-Gloucester line was revealed by Brush Type 4 No D1734 seen on crew training duties at Stroud on 9 June

)4

Z

A68

107

108

(**105**). Immediately behind the locomotive can be seen one of the Hawksworth brake-compos in chocolate and cream livery converted for slip-coach working on the 'Cornish Riviera Express' in the mid 1950s.

Steam remained in control of one main line only after the Cheltenham/Gloucester services succumbed to diesel haulage. The Paddington-Worcester services were scheduled for steam haulage until September 1963, but in fact many trains continued to be hauled by steam locomotives even after that date because the newly allocated 'Hymeks' were redrafted to the South Wales service following the transmission weaknesses of the 'Western' class revealed by the derailment of D1000 in the following month. In 1963 Worcester shed (85A) clearly still took pride in turning out smart steam locomotives for its Paddington expresses if the appearance of 'Castle' No 7004 *Eastnor Castle* photographed leaving Chipping Campden Tunnel (**106**) is any indication, although by the following year it would appear from (**107**) and (**108**) that standards had begun to slip. In (**107**) the appearance of 'Castle' No 7027 *Thornbury Castle* contrasts ill with its appearance two years earlier (**7**) whilst on sister locomotive No 7005 *Sir Edward Elgar* — photographed on 4 July 1964 on the north side of the Hatton Triangle at the head of the 07.45 Evesham-Birmingham — even the BR cast iron smokebox door number appears to have been

10

11

111

removed (probably stolen) and replaced by a temporary painted version. The appearance of 'Castle' No 7025 *Sudeley Castle* seen in (**109**) approaching Evesham at the head of the 13.10 Worcester-Paddington on 29 July 1963 also indicates increasing despondency over steam power and contrasts with the smart appearance of an unusual visitor to the line, BR Standard 'Britannia' class 4-6-2 No 70054 *Dornoch Firth* photographed (**110**) passing the same spot at the head of empty carriage stock in the direction of Worcester on 30 April 1964. It is interesting to compare the customary Western Region steep drop of the up home signal seen in (**110**) with the more modest angle adopted by the same arm in the previous year (**109**).

Although 'Hymeks' had been in use on Worcester services in part since 1963, it was not until May 1964 that the service was totally dieselised. In (**111**) 'Hymek' No D7056 was photographed passing Pershore at the head of the 13.15 Paddington-Worcester and Hereford on 15 August 1963, whilst in (**112**) No D7061 heads the 11.15 Paddington-Worcester through Norton Junction on 13 August 1963. By the following year, when the 'Hymeks' took total control, the smart

112

appearance typified by Nos D7056 and D7061 had given way to the more service-worn aspect of No D7059, photographed (**113**) in Sonning Cutting at the head of the 11.10 from Worcester Shrub Hill on 16 May 1964.

On the same day, the Oxford University Railway Society 'celebrated' the demise of main line Western Region scheduled steam services by running a 'Castle Farewell Rail Tour' from Paddington to Oxford, Hereford, Newport, Didcot and Paddington, at the head of which (**114**) 'Castle' No 5054 *Earl of Ducie* was photographed in Sonning Cutting.

After withdrawal of the 'Hymeks', Worcester line trains were hauled by Class 31s transferred from the Eastern Region at the end of the 1960s, one of which (No 5530) was photographed (**115**) shortly after transfer, passing Midgham on a crew training run on 14 March 1969.

114

13

15

Southern Region Take-over

It had been the intention of Western Region management to abolish all steam locomotive working (other than on the narrow gauge Vale of Rheidol line) by the end of 1965, but in this they were thwarted, in part at least by their inability to obtain Ministerial consent to closure of the ex-Somerset & Dorset Railway between Bournemouth and Bath.

From 1 January 1963, when responsibility for its lines in the Midlands and North Wales was transferred to the London Midland Region, the Western Region accepted responsibility for all ex-Southern Region lines west of Wilton South, the first station on the ex-LSWR line west of Salisbury. By this Regional transfer, the Western Region inherited the ex-Southern Region main line between Salisbury, Exeter and Plymouth; the numerous ex-Southern Region branches in Dorset and South Devon; the 'Withered Arm' branches in North Devon and North Cornwall to Ilfracombe, Torrington, Bude and Wadebridge; and the Southern section of the unique (mainly single-track) ex-LSWR and MR joint Somerset & Dorset Railway. It was not a rich inheritance.

During the first 18 months, little change took place in traditional ex-Southern Region services. Class S15 4-6-0 goods locomotives continued to haul goods traffic, particularly ballast trains from Meldon Quarry at Okehampton, as they had in SR

11

11

118

days when Class S15 No 30831 was photographed approaching Templecombe with an up freight from the West Country on 4 November 1961 (**116**); Class N and U1 2-6-0s remained the mainstay of passenger and goods traffic in North Devon and Cornwall, on which work Class N No 31821 was photographed on 5 June 1964 at Lapford at the head of the 13.10 Barnstaple-Exeter pick up goods (**117**); while Bulleid Pacifics performed on both fast and semi-fast services. In (**118**) 'West Country' 4-6-2 No 34097 *Holsworthy* is seen approaching Semley on 28 April 1962 at the head of the 06.15 Plymouth-Salisbury formed of a three-coach ex-Southern Railway set and ex-Southern Railway parcels van, whilst unrebuilt 'West Country' No 34106 *Lydford* is seen in (**119**) accelerating away from Sherborne with an up express for Waterloo during the summer of 1963, hauling a rake of BR standard coaches in Southern green livery. Even the 'Atlantic Cóast Express', the Southern Region's crack express which had been accelerated to enjoy a mile-a-minute schedule between Waterloo and Salisbury in the summer 1961 timetable and whose time to Exeter was only bettered by the 'Cornish Riviera Express' after the Western Region decelerations in 1962, continued in operation, hauled between Waterloo and Exeter Central by Bulleid 4-6-2 'Merchant Navy' Pacifics.

On the branch lines in South Dorset and South Devon ex-

119

120

121

122

LSWR Class M7 0-4-4Ts (introduced in 1897) steamed on, as illustrated (**120**) by No 30052 photographed approaching Yeovil on 16 March 1963 at the head of the Yeovil Junction-Yeovil Town auto-train.

If the Western Region took over nominally at the beginning of 1963, it can be said to have been seen to have taken over by 1964. The biggest change took place on the main line in September 1964. On Sunday, 5 September, the last day through trains were run between Waterloo and destinations in North Devon and Cornwall, and on the following day the WR introduced a revised 'Warship' diesel-hauled semi-fast service between Waterloo and Exeter St Davids only. Under the new service, fast trains were scheduled to leave Waterloo at 09.00, 11.00, 13.00, 15.00, 17.00, 18.00 and 19.00, all of which ran through to Exeter St Davids except the 11.00 (the former 'Atlantic Coast Express') which terminated at Salisbury with a connection thence on the retained Brighton-Plymouth through service. With minor exceptions, all trains called at Woking, Basingstoke, Andover Junction, Salisbury, Gillingham, Templecombe, Sherborne, Yeovil Junction, Axminster and Sidmouth Junction. Although the best new time for the overall journey was 3hr 35min (as compared with the former 'Atlantic Coast Express' best time of 2hr 58min) the average times from Waterloo to Exeter improved and many intermediate stations enjoyed a substantially improved and accelerated service to the capital. 'Warships' had, in fact, been introduced to a number of ex-Southern Region services on 17 August before the introduction of the new timetable, including the up 'Atlantic Coast Express'. Despite initial 'teething troubles' the interval semi-fast service on the ex-LSWR main line found general acceptance with the travelling public and has managed to survive into the 1980s, albeit with considerable track rationalisation involving the single-tracking of the greater part of the line between Salisbury and Exeter. In (**121**) Class 42 No D816 *Eclipse* is seen heading the 13.00 Waterloo-Exeter St Davids on one of the single-track sections near Buckhorn Weston Tunnel (near Gillingham) in August 1968; and in (**122**) No 807 *Caradoc* stands at Exeter Central in September 1969 awaiting departure on the 14.33 Exeter St Davids-Waterloo. After the withdrawal of the 'Warships', the Waterloo services were powered by Southern Region Class 33 locomotives, until these were in turn replaced by Class 50s rendered available by increasing numbers of HSTs for Paddington-West of England services.

'Westernisation' of the branch lines also proceeded apace. The M7s on the Yeovil Town — Yeovil Junction branch (**120**)

123

12

25

were replaced by ex-GWR auto-fitted 0-6-0PTs, one of which, No 6435, was photographed on 18 July 1964 at the head of the 15.50 Yeovil Junction-Yeovil Town (**123**), and subsequently by four-wheel railbuses (**124**) which were also used on the ex-LSWR branch to Bodmin North. On the Axminster-Lyme Regis branch, the 1882-built Adams 4-4-2Ts Nos 30582/3/4 (**125**) were replaced by non-Southern locomotives before the inevitable closure of the branch in November 1965 and in (**126**) LMSR-designed 2-6-2T No 41291 hauls an ex-GWR auto-coach across Cannington Viaduct on the 11.42 Lyme Regis-Axminster on 6 March 1965. On the Seaton branch, which closed on 7 March 1966, the traditional M7s were replaced towards the

26

12

12

end by ex-GWR 0-4-2T locomotives, one of which, No 1442, was photographed (**127**) near Colyton propelling the 10.20 Seaton-Seaton Junction auto-train also on 6 March 1965.

On the ex-Southern Region 'main lines' west of Exeter, dieselisation of services was all but completed by the time of the introduction of the new 'Warship' timetable to Waterloo, diesel power being provided by 'Hymek' Type 3 and NBL Type 2 locomotives, 'Warships' and diesel-mechanical multiple-units. The use of Western Region locomotives on the Plymouth-Okehampton-Exeter section was not unprecedented, as the Western Region and Southern Region (and the Great Western and Southern Railways before them) had long rostered workings of locomotives and crew over each other's lines for route learning purposes. In (**128**) Laira-based green-liveried 2-6-0 No 7335 pulls a Southern Region 3-coach set away from Okehampton in April 1960. It was particularly important for Western Region crews to have knowledge of the Southern Region route between Exeter and Plymouth, because it was over this route that Western Region trains were diverted whenever the coastal section of Western Region main line near Dawlish suffered storm damage.

Although through coaches from London for the Southern outposts such as Bude, Padstow and Torrington disappeared with the new 1964 timetable, summer holiday traffic was still considered sufficient to justify the provision of through trains between Paddington and Ilfracombe in 1965 and 1966, hauled by 'Warships' or 'Hymeks', and non-dmu services were regularly provided between Exeter and Ilfracombe and Exeter and Plymouth (via Okehampton). In (**129**) a smart Hymek No D7095 — showing off the pleasing appearance of the two-tone green livery initially adopted for the class — leaves the terminus at the head of the 10.20 Ilfracombe-Exeter train on 22 July 1964; and in (**130**) 'Warship' No D812 *Royal Naval Reserve 1859-1959* passes a Class 22 locomotive in the siding at the approach to Barnstaple Junction on 12 August 1968. Most other services on the ex-Southern Region 'withered arm' were provided by

29

30

13

13

multiple-units. In (**131**) a 3-car Swindon-built cross-country unit approaches Barnstaple Junction on a service from Bideford on 2 September 1969, shortly before the withdrawal of passenger services between Torrington and Barnstaple Junction, and in (**132**) a mixed unit of suburban and cross-country stock is seen near Heddon Mill Crossing on the approach to Ilfacombe three days earlier, on 31 August. Services between Ilfracombe and Barnstaple Junction were withdrawn in October 1970.

On the ex-LSWR Exeter-Plymouth main line, all services were withdrawn between Bere Alston and Okehampton — and the alternative route so important in the event of storm damage at Dawlish abandoned — in May 1968, although a truncated service survived between Okehampton and Exeter for a further four years. In (**133**) Pressed Steel single-unit motor brake second No W55029 enters Okehampton station from the west to form the 14.35 to Exeter St Davids on 3 April 1969. The line between Crediton and Okehampton remains in situ for ballast traffic from Meldon Quarry (immediately to the west of Okehampton), and the Torrington branch and part of the former North Devon and Cornwall Junction branch remains in use for goods traffic as far as Meeth. On this line, opened as late as 1925, Class 22 No D6334 was photographed at Petrockstow on 14 October 1969 (**134**).

33

◀34

The Somerset & Dorset

The ex-Somerset & Dorset Joint Railway was probably one of the least welcome elements of the Western Region's inheritance from the Southern Region on 1 January, 1963, (the section north of Templecombe had been a WR responsibility since 1958). At the time when the Western Region was pursuing a policy of rapid dieselisation, interval timetable planning and intensive stock utilisation, Western Region management no doubt resented the arrival of an uneconomic, steam powered, mainly single-track railway with which it had few historical links. The S&D cut across the grain of the Western Region, both physically and metaphorically, and little time was lost in seeking Ministerial consent for closure. Through trains from the north to Bournemouth — including the 'Pines Express' — were withdrawn on Saturday, 8 September 1962, and all passenger services were finally withdrawn from 7 March 1966 after the proposed closure in January of that year had been delayed by the absence of adequate alternative road transport.

135

136

137

The S&D in pre-Grouping days had been operated jointly by the London & South Western Railway and the Midland Railway, and the influence of both railways remained strong even a dozen or more years after nationalisation. Although a few BR Class 5 Standard 4-6-0s had been introduced in the early 1950s, of which No 73052 — photographed in (**135**) entering Sturminster Newton on 4 September 1964 at the head of a Bournemouth-Bristol train — is an example which spent many years on the line, the majority of locomotives were still of LMS or SR origin. In (**136**) ex-LMSR Class 2P 4-4-0 No 40700 double-heads a Birmingham-Bournemouth express between Chilcompton and Binegar on 9 September 1961, whilst in (**137**) BR Standard Class 4 4-6-0 No 75027 partners an ex-SR rebuilt 'West Country' 4-6-2, No 34039 *Boscastle* through Binegar on the same day. Even a few original Somerset & Dorset Railway locomotives survived into Western Region ownership and in (**138**) ex-S&DJR Class 7F 2-8-0 (introduced 1914) No 53805 is seen heading a short goods train beneath the Western Region Yatton-Witham branch at Shepton Mallet in September 1960. Although primarily designed for goods work, these powerful locomotives often saw service on heavy passenger trains during summer months until replaced in the final years of the S&D by the BR Class 9F 2-10-0 locomotives (again primarily designed for goods work) which were introduced after successful trials in March 1960.

The Class 9Fs were probably the most suitable locomotives

138

139

ever to operate on the Somerset & Dorset and it was ironic that they were not introduced until the fate of the line had been all but sealed. In (**139**) Class 9F No 92006 (by now fitted with double chimney) leaves Chilcompton Tunnel at the head of the 07.40 Bradford-Bournemouth train on Saturday, 12 August 1961. The last member of the class, the 'Great Westernised' No 92220 *Evening Star* saw service on the Somerset & Dorset line and was appropriately rostered to haul the last 'Pines Express' on 8 September 1962. After the whole line fell within Western Region control, ex-GWR locomotives saw limited service on the S&D, particularly 0-6-0PTs and Collett 0-6-0s, but they always tended to look rather out of place. In (**140**) Western Region influence is revealed by Collett 0-6-0T No 2204 hauling GWR design non-corridor coaches on the S&D near Shepton Montague forming the 16.00 Highbridge-Templecombe.

140

The Western Region in North Wales

As the ex-Southern Region lines transferred to the Western Region on 1 January 1963 have been illustrated in this album, it would be consistent to ignore the section of the ex-Great Western Railway in the Midlands and North Wales transferred to the London Midland Region at the same time. However, as ex-GWR locomotives continued to operate on these transferred lines after 1962 I hope it will not be considered inappropriate for the ex-Cambrian Railways section to be included. Despite the London Midland Region shed plate (6F) affixed to its smokebox, the Great Western origins of 'Manor' 4-6-0 No 7803 *Barcote Manor* photographed in (**141**) leaving Welshpool at the head of the down 'Cambrian Coast Express' cannot be ignored. By 1964 the 'Cambrian Coast Express' was no longer decked in chocolate and cream livery, and it ceased even to enjoy the status of a named train when daily through trains between Paddington and Aberystwyth were withdrawn in March 1967 upon completion of the Euston-Wolverhampton electrification.

During its last years as a steam-hauled express, the 'Cambrian Coast Express' was renowned for the spotless appearance of its locomotives on the Shrewsbury-Aberystwyth section, a reputation fully justified by the sparkling brass work and paint work and the white painted buffers and smokebox fittings on No 7803.

Not all the locomotives in use on the Cambrian section were kept in such spotless condition, but the unkempt appearance of 'Manor' No 7816 *Frilsham Manor* photographed in (**142**) climbing Talerddig bank at the head of the 11.25 Barmouth-Birmingham Snow Hill on 29 August 1964, is more than compensated for by the manifest evidence of its GWR parentage displayed on the tender more than 16 years after nationalisation.

141

142

14

14

145

Continuing Western Region influence after the transfer of the Cambrian section to the London Midland Region is obvious in (**143**). Beneath GW-style lower quadrant signals, Collett 0-6-0 No 2268 in lined (if grubby) green livery stands at Dovey Junction on 4 August 1964 at the head of a Machynlleth-Aberystwyth train made up of ex-GWR stock. Towards the end of steam on the Cambrian lines, however, more modern BR Standard locomotives increasingly took control, as evidenced by the Birkenhead-based BR Class 4 4-6-0 No 75023 photographed in (**144**) leaving Dolgellau on a Ruabon-Barmouth train on Monday 31 August 1964. This class of locomotive enjoyed the distinction of hauling the last 'Cambrian Coast Expresses' on the Cambrian section. In (**145**) No 75021, adorned with commemorative headboard and wreath, passes Westbury (Shropshire) at the head of the last down 'Cambrian Coast Express' on 4 March 1967. From the number of heads protruding from the coaching stock, it would appear that this last steam-hauled 'Cambrian Coast Express' enjoyed more than the average quota of railway enthusiast passengers!

One class of Standard locomotive which saw relatively little use on the Western Region was the Class 4 2-6-4T. A few members of the class were used on the Somerset & Dorset line shortly before closure, and others were introduced on the Cambrian lines towards the end of steam. In (**146**) Class 4 2-6-4T No 80132 pauses to collect three passengers for Aberystwyth at Commims Coch Halt on 31 August 1964. The London Midland Region viewed its Cambrian inheritance with no more sympathy than the Western Region had welcomed the ex-Southern Region 'withered arm' in the south-west, and the major link between Morfa Mawddach (formerly Barmouth Junction) and Ruabon via Dolgellau (**144**) and Bala Junction was closed to all traffic in January 1965.

One small section of the ex-Cambrian Railways survived the decade under new LM management in good heart. Inspired by the success of the privately-owned Talyllyn and Festiniog narrow-gauge steam railways, the London Midland Region continued to develop the tourist potential of the 1ft $11\frac{1}{2}$in gauge Vale of Rheidol branch that had been recognised by the Western Region in 1956, giving it the honour, by the end of the 1960s of running the only regular steam-hauled service on British Railways. In (**147**) VoR 2-6-2T No 7 *Owain Glyndŵr*, by now repainted in BR standard rail blue, hauls a set of coaches in matching blue livery near Rhiwfron Halt in August 1968. From 20 May 1968 the Vale of Rheidol narrow gauge tracks were realigned and the service transferred from the narrow gauge station at Aberystwyth to a bay in the main line station.

14

14

48

Suburban and Branch Services

Although little affected by the introduction of new high-powered diesel locomotives, both the scope and appearance of suburban and branch line services dramatically changed during the 1960s. At the beginning of the decade — pre-Beeching — a large contribution towards the Western Region operating deficit was provided by loss-making branch services. Although no doubt providing a valuable social service to the towns and villages linked by the branch lines, increasing operating costs and blossoming car ownership combined to condemn many branches to oblivion between 1960 and 1965. In many cases, no effort had been made to reduce operating costs by simplification of signalling procedures or staff reduction, with the almost inevitable result that Dr Beeching should propose the withdrawal of services from such lines. One passenger service already under consideration for withdrawal before the formulation of the Beeching report was that between Taunton and Chard Junction, on which service 0-6-OPT No 9718 was photographed at Chard Central on 9 June 1961, a little over a year before the withdrawal of passenger services (**148**). The cost of maintaining the impressive all-over roof and substantial buildings at stations like this must have contributed towards the branch line deficit, for in 1961 the policy of reducing stations to unstaffed status had not yet gained general support. Another passenger service which had been condemned before publication of the Beeching Report was that between Plymouth and Launceston, on which 2-6-2T No 4555 (now preserved) was photographed leaving Lydford on the edge of Dartmoor (**149**). At that time this small Devon village was graced with a station of four platforms, where the ex-GWR Plymouth-Tavistock-Launceston branch connected with the ex-LSWR Plymouth-Okehampton-Exeter main line. Passenger services

49

15

15

152

were withdrawn for the ex-GWR branch in blizzard conditions on 31 December 1962 and the remaining services on the ex-Southern Region line ceased four years later, on 6 May 1968.

It is interesting, if possibly depressing, to speculate whether more lines would have survived the Beeching Axe if earlier efforts had been made to reduce staff, signalling and other costs by economies such as the abolition of full signalling on little-used lines. Full signalling is evident on the Oxford-Fairford branch on which 0-6-0PT No 7445 was photographed (**150**) after arrival at Fairford on the 12.18 from Oxford on 24 September 1960. Such economies might not have been possible on longer secondary lines, such as that between Taunton and Barnstaple on which 2-6-0 No 7333 was photographed at Wiveliscombe on 1 May 1962 (**151**), but the retention of the Central Wales 'basic' railway indicates that some such lines might have been saved by intelligent planning.

The Chard, Launceston and Fairford branches did not survive long enough for economies to be attempted by the provision of diesel multiple-unit trains. One branch line that has survived, despite its condemnation in the Beeching Report, is that between St Erth and St Ives, upon which a Swindon built 3-car cross-country unit was photographed (**152**) leaving St Ives in August 1962, shortly after the abolition of steam on the branch. Although the substantial granite station building at St Ives has subsequently been demolished and the branch reorganised on a 'one engine in steam' basis, it provides a more intensive service than ever before following the success of a 'park and ride' experiment introduced in 1978 to reduce traffic congestion in the narrow streets at St Ives. A new station, Lelant Saltings, had been constructed as a 'park and ride' station, and the branch now enjoys a half-hourly shuttle service throughout the day during summer months.

Even the lower operating costs of dmus did not guarantee the future of many branch lines, and experiments with even smaller diesel rail buses failed to preserve services on little-utilised branches. Diesel railbuses were first introduced on the Western Region on the branches between Kemble and Cirencester, and Kemble and Tetbury. In (**153**) AC Cars Ltd railbus No W79976 was photographed at Tetbury on 19 August 1963, a year before the branch was closed.

153

15

15

55

Diesel multiple-units were also introduced on secondary main line services and suburban services, upon which many still remain in service. They were first used in substantial numbers on the Western Region in South Wales, Bristol and the West Midlands, but even their lower operating costs did not enable the WR to maintain intensive local services during its period of financial stringency in 1961, when passenger services were withdrawn from the Eastern and Western Valleys in South Wales and suburban services in the Bristol area were substantially reduced.

Both high density suburban units and lower density cross-country units were introduced in substantial numbers on the Western Region in the late 1950s and early 1960s, although it was not always possible to understand the basis upon which such units were distributed. In the West Country, for instance, suburban units constructed by the Birmingham Railway Carriage & Wagon Co Ltd were introduced on stopping services in 1960, one of which is seen in (**154**) shortly after delivery on an Exeter-Newton Abbot working, skirting the River Teign; whilst in (**155**) a Gloucester RCW 3-car cross-country unit enters St Anne's Park, Bristol, on the shorter 12.35 Bristol-Temple Meads-Bath Spa working on 15 September 1967.

A Derby-built suburban 3-car unit in use on a suburban service is seen in (**156**); with motor brake second No W50072 leading, the 13.12 from Colwall enters Worcester Shrub Hill on 2 October 1965. The dmu photographed in Devon sports the 'V' marking with which early diesel multiple-units were adorned, while the cross-country unit wears the intermediate partial yellow front that preceded the current all-over yellow that has been adopted for safety reasons.

15

15

Cross-country services between Bristol and Cardiff on the Western Region, and between Weymouth and Portsmouth on the Southern Region were partly provided by multiple-units and partly by locomotive-hauled trains. In (**157**) a 2-car cross-country unit is seen arriving at Grimstone & Frampton on 18 May 1964 while forming the 16.42 Yeovil Pen Mill-Weymouth train; while in (**158**) 'Hymek' No D7024 was photographed on 28 April 1962 passing Dilton Marsh Halt on the climb out of Westbury at the head of a through Cardiff-Brighton train formed of BR standard stock painted in Southern Region green livery. In 1965 the Cardiff-Portsmouth service was changed to diesel multiple-unit working utilising Swindon-built 'Inter-City' units, two sets of which were photographed in (**159**) approaching Hereford on 31 May 1976 with a Crewe-Cardiff train. When the Cardiff-Portsmouth service was again rostered for locomotive-hauled stock, using Southern Region Class 33 locomotives, Class 33 No D6550 was photographed (**160**) passing Lawrence Hill station, Bristol, on the 14.55 Cardiff-Portsmouth on 6 July 1968.

Inter-City multiple-units initially entered traffic on services between South Wales and the Midlands, Bristol and Plymouth but, after 1968, they were also used on outer-suburban services from Paddington. These units were transferred to the Paddington Division to assuage, in part at least, complaints from Western Region commuters whose outer-suburban commuter services had been converted to multiple-unit working on the occasion of a comprehensive timetable reorganisation in 1964.

As Gerald Fiennes has admitted in *I tried to run a Railway,* he made 'a complete hogsnorton of a bull-like rush at the suburban service'. Galvanised into action by research showing the Paddington suburban services to be not only slow and unpunctual but losing over £0.5million per year, he introduced a new service — advertised under the slogan 'Live on a Western Commuterroute' — based on maximum non-stop runs and high utilisation of diesel multiple-units, only to find the service unacceptable to the public, partly because of the unfitness of the dmus employed for the service. Many outer suburban passengers had been accustomed to travel in express stock, and expected the quality of service vividly described by Fiennes: 'At Reading one day I stood gnawing my nails at the leisurely transfer of branch passengers to our already late main line. "Blow your whistle at them," I hissed at the Inspector. "Sir, we do not blow whistles at people from Newbury." The train used to wait for Peter Hope at Pangbourne and George Gouder at Goring. I yearned for Old Joe who used to be porter at Rayleigh many years ago. "It's time to go, Charlie. Two buggers running down the hill. Right away." Much of the business of the Thames Valley we carried in main line trains weighing around 400 tons.'

This suburban debacle took place shortly after the translation of David Pattisson from Plymouth to the London Division and one of his first tasks to restore peace and order to the suburban service and to recover, as quickly and as far as possible, the goodwill of Western commuters by the introduction of more suitable stock such as the Inter-City units. On inner suburban workings, diesel multiple-units had slowly supplanted the traditional suburban stock hauled by Class 61xx 2-6-2Ts

59

60

16

16

between 1959 and 1961, when 3-car Pressed Steel high-density units (with doors to each individual bay) were widely introduced. Two such units are illustrated (**161**) forming the 13.18 Paddington-Oxford service approaching West Drayton & Yiewsley, whilst in (**162**) two similar units form the 12.52 Paddington-Reading General photographed near Maidenhead on 5 March 1965. On the minor branches, as between West Drayton and Uxbridge, single-coach units were introduced; in (**163**) a Pressed Steel motor brake second leaves West Ealing on the 12.22 Ealing-Greenford service on 28 October 1962 in surroundings less rural than those enjoyed by the earlier Gloucester RC&W single unit photographed on 1 September 1964 leaving Maiden Newton on the 13.30 service to Bridport (**164**).

Following the precedent set by the GWR in introducing two streamlined diesel parcels cars (W17/34) in 1936 and 1941 respectively, a number of similar units were introduced as part of the 1959/61 suburban dieselisation scheme by the Western Region, one of which (built by Gloucester RCW) was photographed hauling two general utility vans between Iver and Langley in (**165**).

63

64

65

16

Goods Train Changes

Just as the number of towns and villages served by passenger trains was substantially diminished during the 1960s, so also was the freight service offered by the Western Region reduced in size during the decade of development. In 1960 many of the branch lines that were to receive the kiss of death from Dr Beeching increased the Western Region deficit not only by incurring losses on passenger services but also by providing unremunerative goods facilities. The number of loss-making goods stations may even have exceeded their passenger counterparts, as, in many cases, British Railways continued to provide occasional goods trains even after passenger services had been withdrawn. On the Presteign branch, for instance, passenger services had been withdrawn as long ago as 1951, but goods services continued — over weed-ridden track — until 28 September 1964. In (**166**) 0-4-2T No 1420 was photographed passing Titley Junction at the head of a Presteign goods train on 13 August 1964, shortly before eventual closure. Similarly, the Abbey at Malmesbury saw no scheduled passenger trains after September 1951, but a goods service continued until November 1962. Four months previously, Class 03 0-6-0 diesel shunter No D2188 was photographed at the Malmesbury terminus at the head of the morning freight from Little Somerford on 25 June (**167**). On the ex-Midland Railway branch from Stroud (Midland) to Dudbridge, passenger services had been withdrawn even earlier, in June 1947, but local goods facilities were still provided for another 19 years on the branch, no doubt at a substantial loss if the one-truck load of the local goods hauled by Class 4F 0-6-0 No 44045 on 2 September 1964 (**168**) was a true guide to local demand. Similarly, the economics of the daily goods from Cheddar to Cranmore, photographed on 18 August 1966 hauled by 'Hymek' No D7024 (**169**), would appear to be doubtful.

16

68

69

170

171

172

Whether on minor branch lines or main lines, the majority of goods vehicles in use on British Railways in 1960 were of the old-fashioned short wheelbase type, unsuited for high speed work and often not brake fitted. The lamp code on ex-WD 2-8-0 No 90403 photographed (**170**) entering the closed Broadway station (between Stratford-on-Avon and Cheltenham) on 7 May 1962 reveals the 'unfitted' character of its load, as does the 'express freight or ballast train not fitted with continuous brake' code carried by Class 9F 2-10-0 No 92244, photographed pulling out of Stratford-on-Avon in (**171**) on 28 May 1960. In contrast, sister locomotive No 92137 photographed near Stonehouse (**172**) carries a Class C headcode indicating that its train of Esso tankers is fitted throughout with automatic vacuum brake operative on not less than half the vehicles and illustrates the concept of the company or block train upon which future freight development was largely based. Block coal and mineral traffic has always contributed an important part of Western Region freight income, and a short train of ore wagons was photographed in (**173**) hauled by green-liveried 2-6-0 No 6394 through Hatton on 29 September 1962. Although coal traffic from South Wales has diminished as the nation's appetite for coal has decreased, it still formed an important part of Western Region traffic throughout the 1960s and coal trains in South Wales were hauled after the demise of steam mainly by

173

Class 37 locomotives; D6929 of this class was photographed passing Cardiff General at the head of a train of coal empties in May 1964 (**174**).

On British Railways in general, and on the Western Region in particular, two major consequences flowed from the diminishing use of old-fashioned wagons and the increasing use of block trains. Under the proposals contained in the 1955 modernisation plans concentrated automatic marshalling yards were to be constructed throughout the whole British Railways system to eliminate, as far as possible, the expensive and inefficient 'tripping' workings that were required between the numerous small goods yards (often more than one in a town) originally constructed by pre-nationalisation or pre-Grouping companies. On one such working, 0-6-0PT No 9711 (**175**) was photographed at Gloucester in 1965. On the Western Region, it was proposed that three new yards should be built near Gloucester, Shrewsbury and in South Wales, but only this last yard, at Margam (near Port Talbot) was constructed and Gerald Fiennes has expressed the view in his book that insufficient homework was done as to its location and that Margam 'was clearly wrong'. Margam was opened in 1960 and its location had no doubt being determined by its proximity to the new Margam Steelworks then being developed by the Steel Company of Wales, but it is probable that Margam yard has never operated at full capacity or fully justified the expense of its construction. The flyover at Bishton was constructed as part of the Margam yard scheme.

Even if not fully utilised, Margam yard continues to provide useful facilities for Western Region goods traffic, but the same cannot be said for the (to date) shortest-lived British Railways diesel class of locomotive (Class 14) introduced in mid-1964. This 650hp Type 1 0-6-0 diesel-hydraulic class (of which 56 were eventually built) was built at Swindon Works and was designed and constructed to an essentially WR specification intended primarily for shunting duties and trip working. The closure of local goods yards and the reduction in trip working meant that the task for which the class had been designed had all but disappeared before the first locomotive was delivered, and the locomotives saw but limited use on permanent way duties — on which No D9521 was photographed in (**176**) — and on local goods service before the whole class was withdrawn, less than four years later, in April 1968. In (**177**), newly delivered No D9505 was photographed passing Bristol (Barrow Road) engine shed on 26 September 1964, performing one of the duties for which it was designed. Although the class only saw less than four years service on British Railways, many of its members remain in use on industrial lines.

During the 1960s the foundations were laid for the development of the block trains, company trains and Freightliner trains which make up such a large part today of British Railways

174

175

76

◀77

178

179

and Western Region freight traffic, although during the 'decade of development' itself it is probably true to say that little of the structure above foundation level became visible to the general public. House coal concentration depots were opened at Taunton and West Drayton, and an early (if not wholly successful) Western Region block train experiment was the 'Clayfreighter' introduced between Burngullow (near St Austell) in Cornwall and Sittingbourne in Kent on 23 February 1967. In (**178**) Class 47 No D1670 *Mammoth* enjoys a ceremonial send-off from St Blazey on the inaugural service. The 'Par-Park Royal Freightliner', photographed in (**179**) on 10 June 1969 at Aller Junction hauled by Class 47 No 1596, has also been withdrawn.

180

The Later Years of the Decade

By comparison with the exciting changes that took place on the Western Region between 1960 and 1964, the second half of the 'decade of development' may appear somewhat tame. The changes in the early part of the decade had been dramatic. During a period of only five years the motive power scene had been transformed from steam to diesel, and many long-held Great Western traditions had been abandoned in the effort to recover financial control and to attract public support for a modernised railway. In comparison, the second half of the decade may appear superficially unexciting, but in reality the speed and frequency of Western Region express trains increased slowly but steadily throughout this period to provide the basic and strong base from which the Western Region was able to launch forth, only a few years later, into the HST age of the 1970s. As the total complement of Class 52 'Western' diesel-hydraulics was delivered, and more Class 47 diesel-electrics were introduced, a programme of steady acceleration on all lines was introduced by the Western Region. Class 42/43 'Warships' and Class 52 'Westerns' continued to provide the mainstay of motive power on the West of England main line until the end of the decade, by which time most of the locomotives in those classes had abandoned their maroon livery for standard BR blue. Gleaming in new paint, Class 42 No 866 *Zebra* was photographed (**180**) at Torquay on 14 June 1969 at the head of the 10.50 Paddington-Kingswear (which train includes at least one Mk II open-second coach in its formation); while a month later sister locomotive No 804 *Avenger* was photographed (**181**) climbing away from Aller Junction towards Plymouth on

181

182

183

84

185

14 July 1969 at the head of the down 'Cornishman'. In (**182**) Class 52 No 1007 *Western Talisman* is seen speeding towards Twyford at the head of the down 'Cornish Riviera Express' on 17 April 1969, a little to the west of Ealing Broadway; at this station Class 52 No 1002 *Western Explorer* was photographed two months later (on 7 June 1969), still in maroon livery at the head of an up Paddington express (**183**). These photographs show that, with only a few exceptions, almost all Western Region main line rolling stock had been repainted by 1969 in the new standard British Railways 'blue and grey' livery, thus avoiding the untidy mixed appearance of the trains of earlier years.

Class 52s also continued to provide main line motive power on the Paddington-South Wales expresses — on which No 1017 *Western Warrior* was photographed at Neath General at the head of the 14.00 Paddington-Swansea on 2 June 1968 (**184**) — and on Bristol services, on which No 1006 *Western Stalwart* is seen near Sonning in (**185**) on 23 March 1967. But on these services the 'Westerns' were joined — as deliveries permitted — by increasing numbers of Class 47 diesel-electrics.

18

In (**186**) No D1674 *Samson* was photographed at the head of the 10.20 Swansea-Paddington near the approach to Patchway Tunnel on 2 January 1968, whilst in (**187**) No D1913 heads a substitute for the down 'Bristol Pullman' near Old Oak Common during a NUR go-slow on 4 July 1968.

The guarantee of increased motive power provided by increasing numbers of Class 47s and the full complement of Class 52s enabled the South Wales and Worcester services to be substantially accelerated in 1965, while on the West of England main line accelerated services were introduced in 1965 and again in 1968. In May 1969 it was found possible to provide an hourly service to the West Country and to provide a $3\frac{1}{2}$ hour service between London and Plymouth on limited trains by the relatively simple, if expensive in fuel, expedient of adapting certain Class 42s to work in multiple to provide a total of 4,400hp. In (**188**) Class 42 Nos 822 *Hercules* and 869 *Zest* pass Aller Junction at the head of the 15.20 Penzance-Paddington in June 1969: the mu-fitted locomotives were distinguishable by the diamond markings on the buffer beam clearly visible on recently repainted No 822. Although originally introduced in 1968 on four workings on the West of England main line, multiple-unit operation was reduced to two services in the following year and abandoned as soon as possible thereafter.

These steady but impressive accelerations of services on all Western Region main lines during the late 1960s were sufficient to retain passenger traffic against the increasing competition of the growing motorway system (particularly the M4 and M5) and to provide a sufficiently strong foundation from which the Western Region could build with confidence its unrivalled HST 125mph service now enjoyed by passengers between London and South Wales, Bristol and the south-west.

87

88

Photo Credits

W. J. V. Anderson 85(B)
B. J. Ashworth 24, 46(B), 100(T)
M. H. C. Baker 26
M. Barratt 66(T)
J. C. Beckett 79(T), 86(B)
J. R. Besley 74(B)
P. Bridgman 103(T)
British Rail 22(B), 27(T), 27(B), 100(T)
A. H. Bryant 38(T)
D. E. Canning 73(B)
D. H. Cape 27(B)
J. Clarke 61(B)
G. P. Cooper 108(T)
J. H. Cooper-Smith 19(T), 34(B), 108(B), 111(T)
D. Cross 68(T), 86(T)
H. Daniel 33, 39(T)
M. Edwards 47, 81(B)
English Electric 48(B)
M. J. Esau 68(B), 80(B)
P. J. Fowler 95, 97(B), 110
M. J. Fox 14(B), 64(T), 78(B), 91(T)
E. T. Gill 41(B)
G. F. Gillham 20(B), 83(T), 107(T)
J. Goss 104(B)
P. W. Gray 94(T)
B. A. Haresnape 28(T), 31(B)
H. K. Harman 11(T), 53(T), 54(T), 54(B)
F. A. Haynes 11(B)
C. S. Heaps 21(B), 22(T), 93(T)
G. F. Heiron 10(B)
P. Hocquard 49(T)
J. Hodge 49(T)
D. Holmes 92(B)
Ian Allan Library 30, 45(T), 45(B), 52(B), 63, 65(B), 83(B)
G. J. Jefferson 32(T), 33(B)
B. L. Jenkins 44(T)
B. S. Jennings 92(T)
R. N. Joanes 93(B)
P. Kingston 55
J. L. McIvor 109(B)
N. A. Machell 97(T)
J. F. Medley 60
M. Mensing 15, 16, 52(T)
J. D. Mills 76(T)
G. W. Morrison 84(B), 85(T)
J. K. Morton 13(B), 37(B)
A. Muckley 38(B), 84(T), 88(B), 90(T), 101(T)
R. A. Panting 17(T), 88(T)
I. Peters 62(B), 76(B), 107(B)
M. Pope 10(T), 13(T), 18(B), 31(T), 51(T), 56(T), 57(T), 58(B), 61(T), 99(T), 103(B)
J. Reeves 12(T), 90(B)
G. A. Richardson 19(B), 35(T), 74(T), 75(T), 96(T), 98(B)
S. Rickard 29(B), 36(T), 36(B), 37(T), 40(T), 43(T), 44(B), 46(T), 48(T), 49(B), 50(T), 104(T)
L. Riley 77, 106(B), 107(T), 109(T), 111(B)
P. Riley 69(B), 87(T)
R. C. Riley 81(T), 91(B), 100(B)
G. T. Robinson 32(B), 39(B), 67(B), 79(B), 80(T), 87(B)
P. J. Robinson 67(T), 69(T), 75(B)
M. R. Rutherford 42
A. F. Smith 40(B), 41(T), 43(B), 47, 50(B)
J. R. Smith 65(T)
J. Spencer Gilks 99(C)
B. Stephenson 59(T), 59(B), 62(T), 77(T), 89, 98(T)
W. G. Summer 96(T)
A. Swain 20(T)
R. E. Toop 105(B)
R. O. Tuck 14(T)
W. L. Underhay 17(B), 78(T)
A. A. Vickers 23(T), 25(T), 25(B), 58(T), 70(T), 70(B), 71(T), 71(B), 94(B), 102(T), 105(T)
D. J. Wall 28(B)
J. C. Way 29(T)
J. B. Wells 66(B)
P. H. Wells 82(T), 82(B)
D. P. Williams 12(B)
T. E. Willams 102(B)